A Place of Rede

A Christian approach
Punishment and Prison

The Catholic Bishops' Conference
of England and Wales

burns & oates

PUBLISHERS TO THE HOLY SEE

Burns & Oates

The Tower Building   15 East 26th Street
11 York Road   New York
London SE1 7NX   NY 10010

Burns & Oates is an imprint of Continuum Books

www.continuumbooks.com

First published 2004

British Library Cataloguing-in-Publication Data
A catalogue record for this book is available from the British Library.

ISBN 0 08601 2393 6

Typeset by Benn Linfield
Printed and bound by MPG Books Ltd, Bodmin, Cornwall

The degree of civilization in a society
can be judged by entering its prisons.

Dostoevsky

Prison should not be a corrupting experience,
a place of idleness and even vice,
but instead a place of redemption.

Pope John Paul II

Contents

vii   Foreword

1   Summary

6   Introduction

13   Part I: Justice and Mercy

46   Part II: The Individual and Society

68   Part III: Hope and Redemption

100   Epilogue

101   Recommendations

109   Acknowledgements

110   Appendix *Some voluntary organisations helping prisoners and their families*

117   Index

Foreword

By *Archbishop Peter Smith*
How do we treat the victims of crime? Do we treat convicted criminals with the human dignity which is always theirs? Do we believe in the real possibility of human change and transformation? What is the place of prison in the 21st century?

Debates about criminal justice are often marked by exaggeration and prejudice, and conducted in highly emotive terms. It is not unknown for political parties and the media sometimes to play on this prejudice for their own ends. Yet a reasoned and sober debate is vital. This report from our Bishops' Conference Department for Christian Responsibility and Citizenship draws on the central insights of the Gospel and the social teaching of the Catholic Church to offer a distinctive analysis of the current situation and how it might be improved. It is not a formal teaching document from the Bishops, but it is offered as a contribution to promoting the more open and searching debate our society needs to have.

Despite the incarceration of record numbers of men and women in England and Wales, our prisons are not reducing offending behaviour. The Christian anthropology set out in the report shines a powerful questioning light on the penal policies and practices of our society today, and finds some serious flaws. Whilst upholding the need for justice it offers a fresh perspective aimed at a positive outcome for the victim, for society and for the offender. It invites us all to not to dismiss the prisoner as worthless or beyond redemption. Prisoners are people who share a common humanity with us all. It is a flawed humanity, but one carrying always the potential for change.

A Christian approach to punishment and prison is not a soft option. Love is not the same as being lenient. But Love always looks to the good of the other. In terms of penal policy this means taking every opportunity to reform and restore, never resting content with justifications for policy based only on the need to contain, to deter, or to punish.

I wish to thank Bishop Terence Brain and all those who have worked in the extensive research and drafting that went into this document, including our ecumenical partners in the Churches Criminal Justice Forum. I hope the report not only stimulates a deeper reflection about the future shape of penal policy but also encourages more people within the Christian community and beyond to think about whether and how they might become involved in work in this area.

Archbishop Peter Smith
Chairman, Department for Christian Responsibility and Citizenship
Catholic Bishops' Conference of England and Wales
19 October 2004

Summary

Shortly before Sir David Ramsbotham retired as Chief Inspector of Prisons in July 2001, he sat down to write a farewell lecture at the invitation of the Prison Reform Trust. As he wrote, his wife, Sue, who had watched him tussle with the lamentable state of Britain's prisons for six full years, slapped a piece of paper on his desk on which she had written these words:

- If prison worked, there would be work or education for every prisoner.
- If prison worked, we would be shutting prisons, not opening more.
- If prison worked, judges would not be seeing in the dock the same people over and over again.
- If prison worked, we would not be imprisoning more people than any other European country except Turkey.
- If prison worked, fewer mothers would be in prison and fewer children would be in care.
- If prison worked, we would be saving billions of pounds with fewer prisons, fewer care homes and fewer court cases[1]

True justice must produce a positive outcome for the victim, for society and for the offender. It must give every opportunity for criminals to come to terms with what they have done, to recognise their own guilt, and to acknowledge the need for remorse and penitence. In atoning for their past they recognise the human dignity of their victims and they also help to redeem themselves. It must be possible, within such a system, for an offender to make different choices from those that they have hitherto made. And the system must make it possible for that transformation to take place, and be assisted, at every point during the offender's sentence and life thereafter.

Our existing penal system is a long way from meeting such a

1 Quoted in David Ramsbotham, *Prisongate: the shocking state of Britain's prisons and the need for visionary change*, The Free Press, 2003.

description. The prison system, which this year reached its highest-ever recorded number of prisoners, is stretched to breaking point. The terrible overcrowding only underscores the extent to which our penal system — though it pays lip-service to the need for reform and reha-bilitation — is, in practice, essentially punitive. This paper outlines several major concerns and makes a number of specific suggestions to rectify this tendency.

There should be greater concern for the victims of crime and more emphasis on restorative justice which gives victims of crime the opportunity to participate in the administration of justice — and which obliges offenders to make amends to the victim and the com-munity.

Many of those in our prisons have histories of significant vulnera-bility and disadvantage. Justice demands that society addresses the disadvantage of prisoners in education, moral training and lack of family support — assistance in all of which will reduce reoffending. This report recommends the development of a prison system in which there is better education, more drug treatment, more behavioural programmes and better mental health care for the large percentage of prisoners suffering from mental health problems. The current record levels of suicides inside prison show the urgent need for this. Our prison system needs greater bias towards the needs of the vulnerable — women, ethnic minorities, the elderly, and the children of prisoners.

There should be a greater range of prison regimes for different prisoners.

Society should take a more constructive attitude to work in prison, and a more normal working day for prisoners should be introduced. The current definition of a full working day in a prison workshop is four hours — of mainly low-skilled menial tasks. This pays scant respect to the dignity of the prisoner and is ineffective in helping prisoners reform their attitude, acquire a work ethic or gain new skills. A full working day should be introduced to parallel that of the outside world, eight hours a day, five days a week. The quality of work too should relate to the outside world; with prisoners learning the disciplines and skills they will need when they return to society.

Prison regimes should treat prisoners less as objects, done to by

2

others, and more as subjects who can become authors of their own reform and redemption. In that spirit, the right to vote should be restored to sentenced prisoners.

Prisoners have the right to continue to protest their innocence in prison. The Government should re-examine the tendency of the parole system to deny early release to those who refuse to "show remorse" for a crime which they maintain they did not commit.

Moves should be made to implement the strategy of smaller, more human-scale community prisons outlined by Lord Woolf, so that prisoners serve their sentences in small institutions, integrated into their local community, as close to their homes as possible. This would be both more humane and would, all research shows, reduce reoffending. It would also alleviate pressure on overburdened staff.

Visitors to prisons detect a dispirited workforce – and statistics on stress, sickness and staff turnover reflect this. Undoubtedly some of the workforce in our prisons, including at leadership levels, needs renewal. It is important for the authorities to root out those elements within the prison staff whose vision has been corrupted or jaundiced to the extent that it constitutes an impediment to change. And yet at all levels the prison service has some remarkably dedicated staff for whom the term prison "service" has real meaning. Exemplary public servants in this sector should be identified, listened to and cherished. Society must show a greater duty of care to those who work in our prisons.

Above all there need to be fewer people in prison. The Sentencing Guidelines Council needs to gear its work towards reducing sentence lengths, and reducing the number of short-term prisoners. It needs to divert low-risk offenders from prosecution. It needs to reduce the number of prisoners remanded awaiting trial. It needs to seek alternatives to prison for the large numbers of people jailed for comparatively trivial offences like shoplifting. It needs to counter the inflationary pull which is built into the present system of sentencing.

The automatic progression from fines to community sentences to imprisonment should be re-examined. There should be a far wider range of community service and punishment orders, along with improved drugs treatment programmes. The fines system should be bolstered and revised, with the introduction of Day fines and an end to the fines as the first option for dealing with poor people.

The use of tagging and electronic surveillance should be extended. There needs to be a new flexibility in mixing prison and community punishment in a single sentence – with halfway houses, weekend prisons, individual curfews, exclusion orders and other innovations to assist in the balance between justice and mercy, human dignity and what the common good requires. The Government has gone some way towards this but needs to guard against dangers in its new Custody Plus, Intermittent Custody and Custody Minus sentences which may increase, rather than decrease, the numbers in prison.

For too long there has been a tendency to consider prison as the ultimate backstop for all society's problems – the ultimate social service which must cope with the failures in the work of other departments of government, particularly with regard to mental health, drug and alcohol misuse, housing, employment and social welfare. This must stop. Prison must not be a dustbin for the problems society fails to address elsewhere. The key to making significant reductions in the level and impact of crime lies as much in the development and implementation of wider social and economic policies as it does in reforming the prison system.

There needs to be a change in attitudes within the Catholic Church towards those in prison. As a Church we have to acknowledge that concern for those in prison is – despite it being one of the baldest of Jesus's commands as to how his followers are to serve him[2] – is not at present high up the agenda of many Christians. On this we all need to examine our consciences. There also needs to be a similar change in our wider society. Politicians and the media must treat issues of crime and punishment more responsibly. Those television entertainment executives, newspaper editors and politicians who seek to reinforce prejudices, rather than convey the overall truth, should be held publicly accountable for their actions.

On the detail of all this others may disagree or see other possibilities. Our Christian anthropology insists that the innate dignity and

2 "I was in prison, and you visited me." Matthew 25:36.

worth of each person is not negotiable. Jesus invites us to see himself in the marginalised, alienated and rejected. Thereby he calls us always to extend his Kingdom of mercy and compassion. That call requires us to commit ourselves to a pursuit of justice which is always within the horizon of grace.

The image of God comes to its glory in each one of us. Through justice and mercy, hope and forgiveness, no one is beyond the reach of God's purpose. The possibility of change is ever-present. Society should never give up on any individual. For every place is a place of redemption.

Introduction

Modern man often anxiously wonders about the solution to the terrible tensions which have built up in the world and which entangle humanity. And if at times he lacks the courage to utter the word "mercy", or if in his conscience empty of religious content he does not find the equivalent, so much greater is the need for the Church to utter this word, not only in her own name but also in the name of all the men and women of our time.[3]

Pope John Paul II

1.   Nobody wants to know about prison. It is the concern of those behind bars, those who detain them, the members of their families, and a handful of campaigners and professionals. But as a society the rest of us want, metaphorically, to throw away the key. Yet the issue is not without outside scrutiny. Every prison is visited by a Catholic chaplain, as well as other chaplains, at least once a week and many have a daily witness. The Church has an unbroken history, through the centuries and across the world, of visiting those in prison. In England and Wales, the Catholic Church plays a leading role in the Churches' Criminal Justice Forum, through which Christians of all communities are encouraged to embrace criminal justice as a cause for concern. The Church's locus here is not just that of its moral and social teaching but its experience: Catholic priests spend a considerable part of their ministry dealing with people who fall through the holes in our society.

2.   All this is not an aspect of the Church's social action to which attention is normally drawn, but this report does so now because the overall state of the nation's prisons is a scandal – and the situation has deteriorated rapidly and steadily in recent years. And this is a crisis to which we believe the Church has an important viewpoint to bring, not merely from the perspective of our social concern but because

3 Dives in Misericordia, 15.

Christian theology has important insights to offer into questions of criminal justice, the rights and responsibilities of individuals, and the wider duty of our society to promote the flourishing of all its citizens.

3.   In 2004 the prison population in England and Wales reached its highest-ever recorded level. In April 2004 it stood at 75,544 – an increase of 2,993 over the previous year. It has almost doubled from the 1991 figure of 42,000. The number of women in prison has risen particularly dramatically; ten years ago the female prison population was 1,811; in March 2004 it was 4,549 – an increase of 151%. The rate of imprisonment for black people is now seven times that of the white population. The number of juveniles has doubled over the last decade.[4] The number of elderly men (over the age of 60) has trebled since 1995.[5] On occasions prisons have been so full that had 200 more offenders been jailed there would have been nowhere to put them.[6] The figure has fallen slightly since, and in the last three months has stabilised at just below 75,000.[7] By the end of the decade Home Office projections predict a prison population of anything between 91,400 and 109,600 – though the Home Secretary, David Blunkett, has hinted that he hopes the number will be capped at 80,000 by 2009,[8] an aspiration which may well prove to be over-optimistic.

4.   The result is terrible overcrowding. By the Government's own admission 82 of the 139 prisons in England and Wales are officially designated as overcrowded.[9] Some 17,000 prisoners – 23% of the

4 Youth Justice Board. In 2002 only a quarter of children in prison had been convicted of violent offences. The majority, just over a third were convicted of property crimes such as burglary and theft.

5 Statistics from *Current issues in Penal Policy*, Paul Cavadino, Chief Executive, Nacro, March 2004.

6 "Headroom between the prison population and the maximum useable accommodation in the whole prison estate [was] less than 200" HM Prison Service, 2004, quoted in *An analysis of the Prison Service's performance against its Key Performance Indicators 2003-2004*, Prison Reform Trust, August 2004.

7 To 74,751 as at 15 October 2004.

8 *Changing Lives, Reducing Crime* – Home Office response to the Carter Report, January 2004.

9 Prison Service *Monthly Bulletin – September* 2004, London.

prison population – were recently revealed to be doubling up in cells designed for one.[10] Shrewsbury Preston Prison was recently holding 625 prisoners in cells designed to hold 324.[11] In the last ten years 12 new prisons have opened but nine of those are overcrowded already.[12] As a result record numbers of inmates are committing suicide,[13] drug use is widespread[14] and purposeful activity such as education, employment or exercise for each prisoner is declining. Many prisoners are still locked up for most of the day.

5.   Money is going into expanding rather than improving the prison system. Yet building new prisons has not been a solution: in the last 10 years, 12 new prisons have been opened. Of these, nine were already overcrowded by June 2004. Overcrowding means individual prisoners are facing cuts in their access to prison education budgets and programmes to reduce reoffending. More prisoners are placed far from home, with a deleterious impact on family relationships. Some offenders no longer attend their own cases in the Court of Appeal because they fear that, by the time they return to prison, the cell which they have made their home will have been allocated to another inmate. Overcrowding is such that prisoners are forced to defecate in front of one another and on some prison wings slopping out has been brought back.[15] Our prisons are becoming a public disgrace.

6.   The cause of all this is tougher sentencing by magistrates and judges in response to the Government's more prescriptive sentencing

---

10 Oral evidence to Home Affairs Select Committee on 25 May 2004.

11 Prison Service Monthly Bulletin – May 2004, London.

12 Prison Service Monthly Bulletin – May 2004, London.

13 The highest number of suicides ever recorded in a single month was in August 2004, The Independent 3 Sept 2004.

14 Drug dealing in prisons appears to be becoming much more organised, according to a speech given to the Prison Service annual conference in 2004 by its Director-General, Phil Wheatley. Drug tests inside prison show that as many as 35% of prisoners are using drugs, though many suspect that the real rate is much higher, since only 5-10% of the prison population is tested each month. Last year the figure rose.

15 Written parliamentary answer, 10 5 2004, Hansard 8 June 331w.

guidelines and a climate of increased public intolerance, fed by harsher rhetoric from politicians and media reporting which is often far from responsible. The number of offenders arrested, cautioned and appearing before the courts has remained relatively constant and there has not been any increase in the overall seriousness of offences brought to justice, yet more people are being sent to prison, and for longer. Ten years ago one defendant in 26 would have gone into custody – today the number is double that.[16] Those appearing in magistrates' courts are three times more likely to go to prison than they would have ten years ago.[17] First-time offenders are far more likely to go to prison. This year, for the first time, more than half of all sentenced men in prison are serving four years or more.[18]

7.   This increased severity is a peculiarly British phenomenon. Comparisons with our European neighbours are unedifying. This country has 141 prisoners for every 100,000 of our population – far higher than the majority in Western Europe. Holland has 100, Germany has 98, France has 93 and Denmark has 64.[19] Of the major developed countries only the United States has proportionately more people in jail. There are more life-sentence prisoners in England and Wales today than the whole of the rest of Western Europe added together[20] yet there is no evidence of a higher homicide rate in the UK than in other Western European countries.

8.   These developments are alarming for two reasons. The first is that there is no sign that this increased severity is making our society

16 Factfile, Prison Reform Trust, March 2004.
17 The Carter report: *Managing Offenders, Reducing Crime*, Patrick Carter, Correctional Services Review, December 2003.
18 According to the Director-General of the Prison Service, Phil Wheatley, in *Sentencing policy and the prison population*, (unpublished). As of August 2004 there are more than 24,000 men in his jails (56% of all prisoners) who will be there for four years or more.
19 *World Prison Population List*, Findings 234, Home Office RDS Directorate, 2004.
20 Sir David Ramsbotham, former Chief Inspector of Prisons, *Prisongate: the shocking state of Britain's prisons and the need for visionary change*, The Free Press, 2003.

better or safer. Only 5% of that 30% fall in crime is attributed by the Government to the increase in the prison population.[21] Since some 58% of all prisoners are reconvicted of a further offence within two years of leaving prison (and this figure is even higher for young prisoners, 72% for 18- to 20-year-olds, and 84% among those under 18) the costs are rising rather than falling.[22] Released prisoners, it is estimated, commit at least a million offences a year. The cost to the nation is £11bn a year, according to the Government's Social Exclusion Unit. And that is on top of the annual £3.2bn which the prison system costs our society – an increase of £900m in the past seven years.[23] This inescapably leads to the conclusion that prison doesn't work.

9. But secular campaigners and policy-makers have addressed these issues, and the need for society to achieve a just balance between the respective needs of victims of crime, offenders, offenders' families, and the wider community. In addition to the Social Exclusion Unit report (*Reducing reoffending by ex-prisoners*, July 2002), there has been the Carter Report (*Managing Offenders, Reducing Crime*, December 2003) and a host of informed responses from bodies such as Nacro, the Prison Reform Trust and the Howard League for Penal Reform. The Catholic Bishops' Conference of England and Wales has sought to contribute to public debate on specific issues through the reports *Women in Prison* (published in 1999) and *People, Punishment and Prisons* (2002) which looked at practical questions of policy.

10. It is not the purpose of this report to rehearse these here. Rather it is to concentrate on the second of the areas of concern regarding the present state of the nation's prisons. It is to ask how these should be reformed, not in the light of utilitarian considerations, but in the context of a Christian anthropology which inquires by what right our society deprives people of their liberty – and asks questions about what implications the values of the Gospel have in issues of punishment.

21 Research by the Prime Minister's Strategy Unit highlighted in the Carter report: *Managing Offenders, Reducing Crime*, December 2003.

22 Social Exclusion Unit report, *Reducing reoffending by ex-prisoners*, July 2002.

23 *Changing Lives, Reducing Crime* – Home Office response to the Carter Report, January 2004.

11.   The discussion needs to be deepened and grounded in the foundations of Catholic theology which has something distinctive to offer to the debate on how our prisons should be made better places. Care must be taken to avoid confusion in the application of theology to law, for not everything sinful is illegal in the judgement of the state (nor, conversely is something necessarily immoral because it is against the law, especially where a law may be unjust). Nonetheless, it is not accidental that religious language is so often used in our discussions of crime and punishment because theology rightly underpins our approaches to these vital concerns. Yet how well-informed is the application of that theological vocabulary?

12.   The scriptural basis for the Church's approach to prisoners is well-known: "I was in prison and you visited me,"[24] St Matthew tells us Jesus will say on the day of judgement. But the life of Christ itself offers its own commentary. In the paraphrase of one prison campaigner: Jesus was arrested in the middle of the night on the word of a paid informer, subjected to intimidating questioning, and remanded in custody, after which he was subjected to police brutality, given a bogus trial and then condemned to die by a weak judge who was put under pressure by public opinion.

13.   There is, of course, far more to it than that. The Gospels give to the Christian community a privileged insight into the constitution and destiny of humanity and God's presence in the world. A central part of their revelation is that love of God and love of neighbour are not to be separated; indeed, Jesus treats them not as two discrete acts but as one act. The command to "love our neighbour as ourselves"[25] tells us that others cannot be treated as accidental to our self-understanding and realisation. There runs a communion of goodness through all created things. Men and women are not redeemed unless all of our relationships are also redeemed.

24 Matthew 25:41-43.
25 Matthew 22:37-40; Luke 10:27.

14. The reality and the logic of the Incarnation forbids an easy dualism between Christians and the world. Rather it calls Christians – individually and as a Church – to be constantly engaged in a creative interpretive witness to the values of the Kingdom which is to work for the common good of all. This is not a one-way process. The values of society will offer significant opportunities and insights and realise values that may be recognised and accepted by Christians as their own – for the Spirit works in all things and builds upon goodness, wherever it is to be found. To live the Christian life well is to mediate between a society whose ends are not governed by the Gospel and a vision which is shaped by Christ and God's salvific purpose for all human beings. Only by doing that will society find new ways out of the disarray, failure and moral neglect which constitute the life of our nation's prisons.

15. In 2001 The Catholic Bishops of England and Wales asked:

"With prison populations rising fast, and rates of reoffending on release very high, is there not an urgent need, without compromising public safety, to consider how best to educate and rehabilitate prisoners rather than just contain them? At present it is quite clear that many of them are not being treated with the dignity and respect which is theirs as human beings. The prison population is higher per head of population than in any other European country. Do they all need to be in prison? Should not other solutions be urgently and carefully explored?"[26]

In the interval things have only got worse, and the questions have remained unanswered.

26 *Vote for the Common Good*, Catholic Bishops' Conference of England & Wales, 2001.

I: Justice and Mercy

The story of Frank Cook (part I)

He was at one point Britain's "most wanted man". His name was Frank Cook, a former armed robber and gangland 'enforcer' in South Yorkshire. He was incarcerated for over half of his life, wreaking havoc in every prison in which he was locked up.

It had begun with a string of convictions starting in his childhood, resulting in lengthy spells in children's homes, approved schools, detention centres and borstals. As a youth almost all his family and friends were thieves. The more he stole, the more he got patted on the shoulder by his peers. The only way that he had to be "normal" was to drink, use drugs and commit crime. He was sent to a youth detention centre but it did little to alter his behaviour; instead it provided what he later called "the biggest launch" in his career as a criminal. All he learned there was "that I could take pain — I came out of there fit, thick, homeless and anti-social with no sense of direction." The pull of belonging meant that he inevitably went back into crime.

He was not a man, perversely, without ambition. "I wanted to be the best gangster. I worked hard in the gym and I challenged people to fight," he said. He progressed to more serious crimes involving guns, shooting at people and taking hostages. He served long periods in custody where, he said: "I mixed with the worst. Brutality was rife. I shaved my head, went to the gym and thought that people wouldn't hurt me if I was nasty. And that's what I was — nasty, nasty, nasty." He was constantly disruptive, which resulted in him spending long periods in solitary confinement.

It was while in solitary that he was interviewed by Dr Ray Gillett, the Medical Superintendent of Grendon Prison, which had developed radical ideas on the rehabilitation of prisoners through psychotherapeutic treatment. But when Cook was transferred there he continued to cause trouble. One day, after he assaulted some members of staff, he was summoned to see Dr Gillett. He assumed he would be told he would be sent back to the harsher regime of a conventional prison. Instead Dr Gillett put his arm around the recidivist's shoulders. Frank Cook burst into tears ...

A: JUSTICE

16.   Justice is both a personal and an institutional virtue. An awareness of the demands of justice is essential for individuals in their interactions with others. It is also vital at a social level, for without it our civic

institutions would lack credibility and citizens would be reduced to instruments of the state or the controlling power or group.

17.   Philosophers point to two key dimensions to justice – distributive and corrective – but both are about fairness. By "distributive justice" they mean how society allocates the scarce resources for which individuals compete, and how it also distributes the duties and burdens which are also essential to our living well together. By "corrective justice" they mean how the law impartially resolves conflict between individuals and the wrong-doing that this can produce. When it comes to questions of punishment and prison the common assumption is that the issue is essentially one of corrective justice. For society's thinking to be restricted in this way would lead us into a blind alley.

18.   In its most basic aspect justice is encapsulated in the principle of Roman law, *suum cuique tribuere* – to allocate to each his own. In this sense, it has always been closely connected to the ideas of "just deserts" and equality. Rewards and punishments are justly distributed if they go to those who deserve them; and where people deserve the same then justice demands equal treatment. This will be considered further when society's various justifications for imprisonment are examined.

19.   However, our present prison regime, geared in practice almost entirely to straightforward punishment, sends out almost two-thirds of prisoners to be convicted of a further offence within the following two years. There are a number of explanations for this. Prison is a place where offenders have deviant social values reinforced by their fellows and may learn new techniques of crime. They receive inadequate corrective psychological training and insufficient education to pick up the basic literacy and numeracy skills they need to "go straight" when they are discharged. Many leave with little money and no job or home to go to. After release some 60% of ex-offenders find themselves rebuffed when they apply for work specifically because they have been in prison.[27]

27 *Current issues in Penal Policy*, Paul Cavadino, Chief Executive, Nacro, March 2004.

20.   All of this gives us pointers to the nature of the problem. It is that justice demands not only certain behaviour from individuals, but also an appropriate response from the rest of society. Although there is a particular need to pay attention to the impact that crime has upon those people who become its direct victims, the central concern must be about the violence which crime does to the common good. But society has to guard against the risk that our attempts to repair any tear in the social fabric may create a fresh one. It is no coincidence that those measures which are known to reduce reoffending – reducing truancy and school exclusion, improving youth employment, tackling homelessness, promoting youth activity programmes, curbing drug and alcohol misuse and promoting measures to support families in distress – are all essentially social rather than directed at the individual. A dialectic between the rights of the individual and the rights of society also seems to be central to any discussion of penal policy.

21.   This takes us onto the question of distributive justice. When it comes to finding criteria for the just distribution of society's benefits and burdens, Christian tradition is clear.[28] It leans away from the notion that what is due to each person is given by laws, customs and shared understandings of the community of which that person is a member. Instead the Catholic approach is rooted in an understanding of creation as being ordered in justice by the Creator. This is normally developed in terms of a concept of "natural law". To act legally is not necessarily to act justly. Rather, it requires that society's positive laws be in accordance with natural law which is known through reason.

22.   The Bible has a particular insight to offer on the question of justice. The Old Testament portrays God as just or righteous. Often the portrait is of God passing judgement on the unfaithfulness of his people. But God's justice is not that of an impartial judge adjudicating

28 See David Faulkner, The reform of Sentencing and the Future of the Criminal Courts, in Rethinking Sentencing, a report from the Mission and Public Affairs Council of the Church of England, Church House Publishing, July 2004.

between the claims of competing or conflicting peoples to achieve peace and harmony. It is manifest also in deeds that liberate the weak and vulnerable from bondage, and which require his people to act in ways conducive to human flourishing. As the Catholic bishops of England and Wales noted in their document, *The Common Good*: "People who are poor and vulnerable have a special place in Catholic teaching: this is what the Church means by the 'preferential option for the poor'. Scripture tells us that we will be judged by our response to the 'least of these', in which we see the suffering face of Christ himself."[29]

23.   The traditional symbol of justice – as a blindfolded woman with a pair of scales – is thus not adequate. Biblical justice and legal justice are not one and the same thing. **True justice must have an inherent bias toward the marginalised, vulnerable or oppressed individuals in society.**

JUSTICE FOR THE VICTIM

24.   A cartoon in the *New Yorker* magazine once depicted two men walking past a man lying dazed and beaten in the gutter. One passer-by says to the other: "Whoever did that must be in need of a lot of help." The sardonic drawing made several points. It reflected the widespread view that the victims of crime are neglected in modern society and that the treatment of criminals is too soft. These are real concerns and no account of crime and punishment can afford to ignore them. This is particularly true of a Christian account which must hold in mind Christ's parable of The Good Samaritan,[30] of which the cartoon was an ironic echo and which in theological terms, points to the needs of the victim as the first imperative.

25.   Support for victims in our society is by no means automatic, and many experience insensitive or inappropriate treatment at the hands of official bodies or others with whom they come into contact. **The lack of transparency in sentencing – whereby an offender**

29 *The Common Good and the Catholic Church's Social Teaching*, Catholic Bishops' Conference of England and Wales, 1996, par 14.
30 Luke 10:25-37.

fairly automatically serves less time in prison than the sentence handed out by judges and magistrates in court – is a source of unnecessary exasperation for some. The Government needs to address this. Official forms of support or compensation are often not sufficient to attend to the needs of many victims. For some victimhood can become a permanent and debilitating state.

26.   The charity Victim Support in 2003 offered assistance to 1.4 million people who had been victims of crime. This ranged from practical help with applying for compensation or getting a broken window repaired to emotional support. It also gave advice on criminal justice processes, but since 97% of crimes never reach court most work on supporting victims needs to be done in other spheres.[31] **Greater awareness of the physical and psychological problems of victims is needed from all citizens, most particularly those who come into contact with victims of crime either through official agencies or as employers, landlords, neighbours and friends.** What victims need, most say, is not more punitive sentences but that their needs are recognised and addressed and that they are treated with greater respect and kept better informed. **Greater awareness of these issues should be encouraged among Christians at parish level.**

27.   In addition to the two dimensions identified by philosophers (see para 36) another promising area, where new approaches are being tested, is in the notion of "restorative justice". Crime damages relationships between people who live in the community. Restorative justice therefore offers victims of crime an opportunity to participate in the administration of justice – and it obliges offenders to take responsibility, requiring them to acknowledge the harm they have caused and work to make amends to the victim and the community. Victims are offered the chance of a meeting with the offender. They can also be given the power to help define the obligations the offender takes on, which may include direct reparation to the person violated.

31 Victim Support briefing, June 2004.

28.   Such an approach has been pioneered by bodies like the Truth and Reconciliation Commission in South Africa whose work, as Archbishop Desmond Tutu put it, saw offences primarily as acts perpetrated against individuals rather than society.[32] In more straightforward criminal contexts the principle of restorative justice is to see crime as a violation of human relationships and to emphasize the intrinsic value in all those involved – victims, perpetrators and criminal justice professionals. In countries like New Zealand, where some of the most long-standing experiments have taken place, a real reduction in reoffending rates has resulted. The British Government has now begun to explore this area, publishing a consultation document in 2003.[33]

29.   This kind of approach embraces many principles of Christian teaching such as right behaviour,[34] repentance,[35] forgiveness,[36] healing[37] and restoration.[38] Most of all, it recognises the value of each and every individual, be that person victim or offender. As Christians, we believe that we are all "offenders" before God, yet are still loved by him.[39] We share a belief that we are all capable of change.

---

32 Desmond Tutu, No Future Without Forgiveness, Rider Books 1999. "Forgiveness is taking seriously the awfulness of what has happened when you are treated unfairly. It is opening the door for the other person to have a chance to begin again. Without forgiveness, resentment builds in us, a resentment which turns into hostility and anger. Hatred eats away at our well-being. In Africa, we have a word, ubuntu, which is difficult to render in Western languages. It speaks about the essence of being human: that my humanity is caught up in your humanity because we say a person is a person through other persons. In our African understanding, we set great store by communal peace and harmony. Anything that subverts this harmony is injurious, not just to the community, but to all of us, and therefore forgiveness is an absolute necessity for continued human existence."

33 Restorative Justice: the Government's Strategy, HMSO, July 2003.

34 John 8:11.

35 Luke 23:39-44.

36 Matthew 6:14-15.

37 Isaiah 61:1-2.

38 Luke 15:11-24.

39 Romans 3:22-24.

30. The virtue of restorative justice is that it can produce a win-win situation. For the offender this can provide the motivation to reform, which the prison system so signally fails to do for many. Through restorative justice the criminal comes to realise that crime generates a history not only for the offender but for the person at the receiving end too. The process can prompt within offenders a recognition of the wrong they have done, and of how this harms not just others but also themselves. This is the first point in a crucial process; from it grows repentance, which couples the act of acknowledgment of wrongdoing with a turning to seek forgiveness. And from that flows the atonement which involves an attempt to make reparation in some way.

31. For the victim it can bring closure on issues of fear, vulnerability, personal security and even self-blame: victims are often dogged by questions like: "Why me?" which can find resolution in meeting the offender or communicating with the offender indirectly through a mediator. Some victims value the opportunity to tell the offender how the crime affected them. Restorative justice is not merely about finding a way for victims and society to forgive an offender; it is about creating a system which recognises that the perpetrator and the victim are members of society who both need reintegrating into something like normality. **This report recommends far greater use of restorative justice models within our nation's penal system.**

32. There are, however, caveats. One is that bringing the victim and the offender together must never become an added pressure or burden for the victim. To make a victim feel an obligation to participate could amount to a revictimisation.[40] Another is that it requires careful moderation if the victim is not to have unrealistic and oppressive

---

40 Victim Support suggests that victims' responses to the suggestion of restorative justice will range from wanting no involvement at all to a variety of levels of engagement – perhaps accepting a letter of apology, asking for and being given information about the crime or the progress of the case, providing relevant information including about the effects of the crime on them, accepting direct practical reparation or suggesting alternative community reparation, indirect mediation or a meeting with the offender. *Victim Support Policy on Restorative Justice in Criminal Justice*, October 2003.

expectations of the offender's obligations. Yet another is that we must be careful never to allow the understandable anger of an individual victim – still less the prejudice of public opinion – to determine decisions. Criminal justice must not be reduced to the whim of a public clamour which so often will be weighted against the marginalised. There is debate about whether restorative justice is best implemented within the state's criminal justice system or as an alternative to it and there are worries in some quarters that restorative justice could become a mere management technique in the hands of an essentially punitive justice system.[41]

33. The point of transforming the individual offender is not primarily to encourage the victim or family to forgive, again notwithstanding how edifying that would be. A distinction must be maintained between the moral duties owed to the victim of a crime by the perpetrator, on the one hand, and the debt incurred to society on the other by the criminal's attempt to superimpose his or her will as against the common good. It is because society is punishing the transgression against the common good, not acting as a wronged individual that we can make some sense of the symbolic nature of punishment.

JUSTICE FOR THE PRISONER

34. In coming to live among us and in dying, without protest, on the Cross, God chose vulnerability. But for many in our society their vulnerability is enforced. Popular opinion would not include in that category the 74,700 men and women who are confined in our nation's prisons today.[42] They are not seen as individuals in need of the love of God so much as people who have been hell-bent on destroying that in the lives of other people. And yet when Jesus, from the Cross, spoke the words: "Today you will be with me in paradise,"[43] he was speaking to a convicted thief.

---

41 See Tim Newell, *Restorative Justice in England*, in *Rethinking Sentencing*, a report from the Mission and Public Affairs Council of the Church of England, Church House Publishing, July 2004.
42 Latest figure: July 2004.
43 Luke 23:43.

35. All the research shows that the men and women in British prisons today are extraordinarily disadvantaged and vulnerable individuals. The Government's Social Exclusion Unit has found that, compared with the general population, prisoners are thirteen times as likely to have been in care as a child, thirteen times as likely to have been unemployed, ten times as likely to have been a regular truant or excluded from school and five times more likely to have been in receipt of benefits. A survey by the Chief Inspector of Prisons showed that two thirds of young prisoners have no educational qualifications and that one in five had no idea where they would live when they left detention. A study by the crime-reduction charity Nacro showed that 60% of young prisoners came from unstable living conditions, 40% had been neglected or abused as children, and that 72% of prisoners had some kind of mental health problem[44] – 14 times the level in the general population. Another showed that 25% of remand prisoners – one in five of whom are subsequently acquitted – had attempted suicide before entering prison.[45] Suicides are a growing problem in our prisons.

36. What such statistics show is that it is dangerous to make assumptions which straightforwardly equate criminality with moral degeneracy – or limit the issue of justice to the determination of guilt or innocence on a particular offence. A full understanding of justice is inevitably more complicated. Where offenders come from broken and impoverished homes and have been reared in an atmosphere of contempt for the police and the law, and whose parents made no serious attempt to keep them in school, the quality of the moral training they received must have been seriously impaired. Rectifying this is one of the roles incumbent on a properly humane prison regime. Yet this is an area in which the present system is notably deficient:

EDUCATION

I. Half of all prisoners are at, or below, the level expected of an

44 *Current issues in Penal Policy*, Paul Cavadino, Chief Executive, Nacro, March 2004.

45 Quoted in *Current issues in Penal Policy*, Paul Cavadino, Chief Executive, Nacro, March 2004.

11-year-old in reading.[46] Two-thirds cannot compete with the average junior-school leaver in numeracy, and four-fifths in writing.[47] One recent inspection found 70% of young offenders (aged 16 to 21) had the reading age of a seven-year-old.[48] Research highlighted by the Government's Social Exclusion Unit has found that prisoners who do not take part in education or training are three times more likely to be reconvicted. By contrast, basic skills learning in prison can contribute to a reduction in reoffending of around a third.[49]

II.   Yet of the £38,000 a year it costs the state to keep an individual in prison — a figure which it has famously been said well exceeds the cost of sending a boy to Eton — an average of just £1,185 per prisoner was spent on education in prison in the year 2002-2003.[50] This is less than half the cost of the £2,590 spent annually on the average pupil in a normal secondary school for the basic education on which many prisoners have missed out. Overcrowding means individual prisoners are facing reductions in their access to prison education budgets and programmes to reduce reoffending. In a city centre prison like HMP Manchester the budget covers only 12% of prisoners.[51] The average number of hours per week prisoners spend on formal education is just six hours.[52]

DRUGS

III.   The number of people in prison as a direct result of drugs is high and growing. Some 16% of male sentenced prisoners were convicted of drug offences in 2002, compared with just 7% in 1993.[53]

---

46 Briefing, Prison Reform Trust, March 2004.

47 Ibid.

48 The Guardian 20 June, 2001.

49 Current issues in Penal Policy, Paul Cavadino, Chief Executive, Nacro, March 2004.

50 Time to Learn: Prisoners' Views on Prison Education, Braggins, J and Talbot, J, Prison Reform Trust, 2003.

51 In July 2004, 23% of prisoners were getting education, but at only half the designated number of hours. Interview with Governor.

52 Prison Statistics England and Wales 2002, Home Office, 2003 (excluding education delivered in workshops and independent study).

53 Ibid.

And there is a much wider group of prisoners whose offence is in some way drug related. Shoplifting, burglary, vehicle crime and theft can all be linked to drug misuse. According to the Government's updated drug strategy, heroin, crack and cocaine users are responsible for 50% of these crimes.[54] Even where there is no direct correlation there is an association: around two-thirds of prisoners use illegal drugs in the year before imprisonment – at least double the proportion of illegal drug users in the general 16–29-year-old population.[55] Alcohol is a serious problem too. The Office for National Statistics says 63% of sentenced male prisoners and 39% of female sentenced prisoners admit to hazardous drinking at a level that carries the risk of physical or mental harm. Of these, nearly half have a severe alcohol dependency problem. These are more likely to be younger prisoners aged 16–24 who have committed violent offences.[56] Yet despite this one city-centre prison visited had only one weekly Alcoholics Anonymous meeting for more than 1,200 prisoners.[57]

IV.   Many prisoners have never received help with their drug problems. The Social Exclusion Unit report estimated that in one prison 70% of prisoners came into jail with a drugs misuse problem but that 80% of these never had any contact with drug treatment services. There are drug treatment and rehabilitation programmes in 60 prisons aimed at prisoners with moderate to severe drug misuse problems but in 2002-2003 just 4,386 prisoners entered these programmes and the target for 2004 was a paltry 5,700 treatments per year.[58] And though nine out of ten young adult prisoners say they used drugs prior to imprisonment only one in three Young Offender Institutions provide drug treatment programmes. Rather, many prisoners continue to get access to illicit drugs while they are inside prison: three-quarters of prisoners admit to taking drugs while

54 *Updated Drug Strategy 2002*, Home Office, 2002.
55 Ibid.
56 *Alcohol and reoffending – who cares?* Prison Reform Trust briefing, January 2004, quoting Singleton, N. 1998: *Substance misuse among prisoners in England and Wales*, Office for National Statistics.
57 Interview with Governor.
58 Briefing, Prison Reform Trust, March 2004.

behind bars, 53% using heroin, and 55% cannabis.[59] Likewise proper treatment and support services in the community for prisoners leaving custody are very limited; where such programmes do exist newly released prisoners often find themselves viewed as "new cases" and have to join the back of the queue.

FAMILIES

v.   A stable, supportive family throughout a prisoner's sentence is a key factor in preventing reoffending, according to Martin Narey, the chief executive of the new National Offender Management Service. "I firmly believe that we should do as much as possible to sustain family relationships at what for many will be an especially traumatic time in their lives," he has written.[60] The Home Office has also acknowledged this: research indicates that good family ties can reduce a prisoner's risk of reoffending by as much as six times.

vi.   Yet many prisoners are still held a long way from their homes. At the end of September 2003, some 26,134 prisoners were held over 50 miles away from their committal court town and 10,880 were held over 100 miles away.[61] On average prisoners are held 53 miles from home.[62] During their sentence 45% of offenders lose contact with their families and many young offenders lose touch with their parents.[63] The number of prison visits has fallen by a third in the past five years despite a rise of over 20% in the prison population.[64] **The Prison Service should add to its Key Performance Indicators one reflecting closeness to home and facilities to arrange visits.**

---

59 *Mandatory Drug Tests in Prisons*, RDS Study 189, Home Office, 1998.
60 Foreword to *Partners in Prevention 2001, Involving Prisoners' Families in Tackling Drug Misuse*, Conference Report, ADFAM National/ HM Prison Service.
61 Briefing, Prison Reform Trust, July 2004 quoting a letter from Paul Goggins, Minister for Prisons and Probation to Annette Brooke MP, 18th December 2003.
62 Prison Reform Trust, 2004.
63 Ibid.
64 *Just Visiting? A Review of the Role of Prison Visitors' Centres*, N Loucks, Prison Reform Trust, 2002.

VII   Meanwhile the recommendations for a new system of smaller community prisons seem no nearer realisation than when they were made by Lord Woolf in his magisterial report on prisons after the Strangeways Riot in 1991[65] – which in the words of the then Conservative Home Secretary Kenneth Baker set out "a blueprint for a humane and riot-free prison system".

VIII.   That insufficient consideration is given by the criminal justice system to the effect of prison on the families of prisoners is a matter for concern. There are a number of issues which need to be addressed, including: the social impact of guilt by association (the very term "prisoners' families" reveals how the spouses and children of offenders are defined by the crime of their family member); the psychological influence on children of having the police arrive to arrest a parent, sometimes in the middle of the night; the cognitive dissonance produced when family members do not recognise the individual described in court as the person they know from home; the tendency of family members sometimes to blame themselves in some way for the offence; and the physical problems of families who find themselves forced to move homes or schools because of the stigma of the offence. **All of these factors should be given more weight by the authorities, and often by the congregations of local churches.**

MENTAL HEALTH

IX.   Many prisoners have significant mental health problems. Some 72% of male and 70% of female sentenced prisoners suffer from two or more mental health disorders. These figures compare with just 5% of men and 2% of women in the general population.[66] Neurotic and personality disorders are particularly prevalent – 40% of male and 63% of female sentenced prisoners have a neurotic disorder, over three times the level in the general population. A significant number of prisoners suffer from a psychotic disorder (7% of men

65 Lord Justice Woolf, *Prison Disturbances April 1990: Report of an Inquiry*, HMSO, London 1991.
66 *Current issues in Penal Policy*, Paul Cavadino, Chief Executive, Nacro, March 2004.

and 14% of women, which is, respectively, 14 and 23 times the level found in the general population). There has been a 77% increase in reported incidents of self-harm amongst prisoners: 17,294 in 2003.[67]

x.   Yet there is a shortage of mental health professionals working in prisons. Only 155 staff, working in 42 mental health in-reach teams, were working with prisoners as of March 2003 – which is the equivalent of one mental health professional for every 322 prisoners suffering from a mental health disorder. Prison regimes do little to address the mental health needs of prisoners; according to the Prison Reform Trust, 28% of male sentenced prisoners with evidence of psychosis reported spending 23 or more hours a day in their cells – over twice the proportion of those without mental health problems.[68] Prisoners with severe mental health problems are often not diverted to more appropriate secure provision. Prison governors are concerned that prisons are being used as a backstop, or "a dustbin" in the graphic phrase of one governor,[69] for individuals who should more properly be in secured mental hospitals. The Chief Inspector of Prisons has estimated, based on visits to local prisons, that 41% of prisoners being held in health care centres should have been in secure NHS accommodation.[70]

37.   The Church must always foster a special concern for the most marginalised. **Within this country's prisons two of the most additionally vulnerable and disadvantaged groups are women and individuals from ethnic minorities. Their situation deserves particular attention for it needs additional redress.**

WOMEN

i.   The number of women in prison has almost trebled over the past decade.[71] Crime by women has not increased, but the severity

---

67 *Safer Custody News*, Prison Service, February 2004.
68 Briefing, Prison Reform Trust, March 2004.
69 Comment to Catholic bishops' representative.
70 *Annual Report of HM Chief Inspector of Prisons for England and Wales 2002-2003*, HMSO, 2004.
71 *Prison Statistics England and Wales 2002*, Home Office, 2003.

with which they are sentenced by the courts has – and even more sharply than the rise in harsher penalties for men. It is not clear why this should be. It may be because of society's stereotype of the woman as carer and nurturer is the more violated by female transgression. It may be because our society does not sufficiently value their caring and parenting role. But the consequence is that women are now generally treated disproportionately harshly by courts. The criminal justice system has begun to discriminate against women.

II.   The increased severity of sentences is significant. A women convicted of theft or handling stolen goods at the Crown Court is now twice as likely to go to prison as in 1991.[72] At the magistrates' courts the chances of a woman receiving a custodial sentence have risen seven-fold.[73] Even more alarming are the punishments being handed out for comparatively trivial offences. In 2003 more women were sent to prison for shoplifting than any other crime.[74] Often women are jailed for motoring offences: in 1991 only 8% of women convicted of motoring offences in the Crown Court went to prison; by 2001 that proportion had increased to 42%.[75] And **it is a matter of deep concern that so many female prisoners are in custody for their financial problems.** Fiscal irresponsibility in individuals should not be condoned, but there must be a better way of supporting and educating individuals and their families out of the downward spiral of debt. **Prison is not the right response save in the most exceptional of cases.**

III.   The kind of women who end up in prison are significantly more vulnerable than their male counterparts. They are 35 times more likely than the general population to be suffering from mental disorders (male prisoners are 14 times more likely, which is bad enough).

72 *The Carter Report: Managing Offenders, Reducing Crime*, Patrick Carter, Correctional Services Review, December 2003.

73 Ibid.

74 *Statistics on Women and the Criminal Justice System* 2003, Home Office, 2004. Just over 2,700 women were received into custody for this offence. They accounted for nearly a third of all women sentenced to immediate custody in 2002.

75 Briefing, Prison Reform Trust, March 2004.

They are seven times more likely to be drug abusers (men are five times). Some 71% of female prisoners have absolutely no educational qualifications. As many as half are estimated to have experienced physical abuse and one in three have undergone sexual abuse. In addition many women prisoners have very limited experience of stable employment; 46% in one survey had not worked in the previous five years. Some 15% of sentenced women prisoners had previously been admitted to a mental hospital and 37% had previously attempted suicide.[76]

THE CHILDREN OF WOMEN IN PRISON

IV.   Women prisoners are much less likely than the general population to be able to call on the support of a stable relationship, but more likely to have childcare responsibilities: 55% of women prisoners have at least one child under age of 16. At least 20% were living as lone parents before imprisonment (compared to 9% in the general population). It is estimated that 150,000 children have a parent in prison.[77] This is a cause for grave concern.

V.   As the *Catechism of the Catholic Church* states:
"The family is the original cell of social life ... Authority, stability and a life of relationships within the family constitute the foundations for freedom, security and fraternity within society. The family is the community in which, from childhood, one can learn moral values, begin to honour God and make good use of freedom. Family life is an initiation into life in society."[78]

VI.   **Depriving children of a family life by sending their only parent to prison is a step which should be avoided in all but the most serious and violent crimes.** Imprisoning women has been shown to have little positive impact on overall crime levels, but it does have extremely negative consequences for families. The majority of women serve very short sentences. In 2002, 40% served a sentence of

76 Ibid.
77 *Every Child Matters*, Department for Education and Skills, HMSO, 2003.
78 *The Catechism of the Catholic Church*, para 2207 (1994).

three months or less, and nearly three-quarters were sentenced to 12 months or less.[79] Few would argue that such short sentences have much of a deterrent effect, nor are they long enough to institute a proper programme of reform. But they are long enough to ensure that around a third[80] of women prisoners lose their homes, and often their possessions, while in prison. And many of the children are taken into care.[81]

VII.   Research by the Home Office shows that 66% of female prisoners are mothers. Each year it is estimated that more than 17,700 children are separated from their mother by imprisonment.[82] Just 5% of women prisoners' children remain in their own home once their mother has been sentenced.[83] As the Second Vatican Council stated: "The role of parents in education is of such importance that it is almost impossible to provide an adequate substitute".[84] **It is impossible to accept that all of these women need to be in prison and all these children deprived of a mother.**

VIII.   Even where children are not taken into care, the system places additional obstacles to the maintenance of close family ties. At the end of 2003 half of all women in prison were held more than 50 miles from their home town. A quarter were held more than 100 miles away.[85] With so many being held a long way from their homes, visits from families are more difficult. One Home Office study found that only half the women who had lived with their children – or been in contact prior to imprisonment – had received a visit since going to prison.[86] All this is in addition to the increased financial, housing,

79 *Prison Statistics England and Wales* 2002, Home Office, 2003.
80 *Psychiatric Morbidity among Prisoners in England and Wales,* Singleton et al, Office for National Statistics, 1998.
81 12% according to *Women in Prison: A Thematic Review* by HM Chief Inspector of Prisons for England and Wales, HM Prisons Inspectorate, 1997.
82 House of Commons written answer 16 May 2003, Hansard.
83 Ibid.
84 *Gravissimum Educationis,* 3.
85 Briefing, Prison Reform Trust, July 2004 quoting a letter to Annette Brooke MP from Home Office Minister Paul Goggins, 18 December 2003.
86 *Reducing reoffending by ex-prisoners,* Social Exclusion Unit, 2002.

emotional and health problems which prisoners' families and children often experience during a sentence.

IX.   It is not even-handed for the courts and authorities to disregard the family dependants of prisoners. This is especially so when it is plain for all to see that it is the mother rather than the father who is the effective carer for children in most single-parent families. To hide behind the protestation that "the law must treat offenders of both genders equally" is disingenuous when this supposedly "evenhanded" treatment results in the punishment of children.

X.   It is not right that the consequences of the crimes of the mothers should be visited on the children. The innocent children of women prisoners should not be especially disadvantaged by the criminal justice system which is carried out in our name. **Immediate steps should be taken by the prison authorities to strengthen the possibility of maintaining ties between women in prison and their children. Judges, magistrates and legislators should be encouraged to find, as a matter of urgency, alternatives to prison for mothers.** It is not acceptable for the authorities simply to ignore this challenge.

ETHNIC MINORITIES

XI.   The rising number of black, Asian and other "non-white" prisoners is a cause for concern, especially since in some prisons there appears to have been a culture of racism over many years. What is particularly alarming is the disproportionate rise in the number of people from ethnic minorities being jailed; in 1999-2002 the general prison population rose by 12% but the number of black prisoners went up by 51%. Black people make up just 2% of the general population but now constitute 12% of prisoners. Some 24% of male, and 31% of female, prisoners are now from ethnic minorities where, if they went pro rata with their representation among the general population the figure would be just 9%.[87] Overall there are 18,000 prisoners from a minority ethnic group and there are now three prisons

87 Statistics from *Current issues in Penal Policy*, Paul Cavadino, Chief Executive, Nacro, March 2004.

where minority ethnic prisoners are in the majority, though there are few staff from ethnic minority communities. There are now twice as many black males in prison as at university. **The Government needs to investigate whether members of ethnic communities are more susceptible to being sent to prison than their white counterparts.** Government also needs new sensitivity to the feeling among many in the Islamic community that Muslim youths, many of them with previously impeccably good character and no police record, received disproportionately harsh sentences after the riots across northern towns in 2001.

38.   To take note of the vulnerability of prisoners' backgrounds is not to excuse moral failure. Sin, as Pope John Paul II says, "is always a personal act ... The human person is free. This truth cannot be disregarded in order to place the blame for individuals" sins on external factors such as structures, systems or other people'.[88] Criminals must be treated as responsible moral agents; not everyone in care, who truants from school, or who takes drugs becomes a criminal. Biblical justice is as clear as legal justice that those who commit crimes cannot escape responsibility for their acts. Punishment is proper and the public as a whole must be protected from such further acts on the criminal's part.

39.   But it must also be stressed that a comprehensive sense of justice requires that the type of punishment should routinely assist all offenders to retake their place eventually in normal society. Where offenders come from backgrounds of vulnerability our society has a duty to help redress those shortcomings. Otherwise we are building what Pope John Paul II elsewhere calls "structures of sin" which "grow stronger, spread, and become the source of other sins, and so influence people's behaviour".[89] Those who cause or support evil, or who exploit it, are of course culpable of sin. But so too, he says, are "those who are in a position to avoid, eliminate or at least limit certain social evils but who fail to do so out of laziness, fear or the conspiracy of silence, through secret complicity or indifference; of

88 *Reconciliatio et Paenitentia*, 16.
89 *Sollicitudo Rei Socialis*, 36.

those who take refuge in the supposed impossibility of changing the world and also of those who sidestep the effort and sacrifice required, producing specious reasons of higher order."[90]

40.   A full sense of justice has to find a way to balance these personal and social aspects and, in doing so, balance the ethical seriousness of sin with the possibilities of mercy, compassion, forgiveness, hope and redemption.

B: MERCY
MERCY IN THE OLD TESTAMENT

41.   Two names for God stand out in the Old Testament. Jewish scholars long ago noted that the two traditions from which these are drawn perceive God to be acting in two distinct ways. The first name, Elohim, which we traditionally translate as God, frames the Divine in terms of justice and the right and faithful ordering of relationships. The second, the Tetragrammaton (YHWH), usually translated as Yahweh, Jehovah or Lord, is associated with God imbued with mercy. In the stories of the Old Testament, beginning with the two different accounts of the Creations in Genesis, it is through both justice and mercy that God is revealed in relationship with the people of the world and with all creation. God discloses that justice alone is not sufficient; it remains incomplete without mercy. Both justice and mercy characterise Israel's experience of God. This is a two-way process. It affects how the people of Israel are shaped by God's actions in history. And it is on the basis of justice and mercy that Israel constantly invokes God's action.

42.   It is to God's mercy that the people of Israel persistently appeal whenever they become aware – often at the prompting of the prophets – of their infidelity in having broken, on many occasions, their covenant with God. It is there at the beginning of the history of the Judges, in the prayer of Solomon at the inauguration of the Temple, in the prophetic work of Micah, in the consoling assurances given by Isaiah, in the cry of the Jews in exile, and the renewal of the

90 *Reconciliatio et Paenitentia*, 16.

covenant after the return from exile. Mercy signifies a special power of love, which prevails over the sin and infidelity of the Chosen People. Without God's mercy, Israel would not exist.

43.   In Jewish and Christian thinking there is thus a profound and continuous tradition which understands both justice and mercy as intimately related and together proceeding from the very nature of God. The calculus of justice can never exhaust all the circumstances and dimensions of human existence. Mercy is the creative response to the limitations of justice because it arises as a genuine act of freedom which can never be coerced or required. It is a sort of excess. True mercy, Pope John Paul II says in the encyclical *Dives in Misericordia* – the Latin of which signifies that God is Rich in Mercy – is "the most profound source of justice".[91] Some theologians affirm that mercy is the greatest of the attributes and perfections of God. It is the mystery of mercy which reveals to us that within history is a sacred history of salvation, a new possibility for being human.

MERCY IN THE NEW TESTAMENT

44.   This experience and witness of Israel finds its expression in the person of Christ. Jesus preached "Blessed are the merciful for they shall obtain mercy"[92] – an axiom which the present Pope has said constitutes, in a certain sense, a synthesis of the whole of the Gospel.[93] He has also made mercy one of the principal themes of his preaching: mercy is at the heart of the parables of the prodigal son,[94] the Good Samaritan,[95] and the merciless servant.[96] But most of all Christ embodied the love of "the Father of mercies"[97] in his death on the Cross which is "the overwhelming encounter of divine transcendent justice with love: that 'kiss' given by mercy to justice".[98]

91 *Dives in Misericordia*, 14.
92 Matthew 5:7.
93 *Dives in Misericordia*, 8.
94 Luke 15:11-32.
95 Luke 10:30-37.
96 Matthew 18:23-35.
97 2 Corinthians. 1:3.
98 *Dives in Misericordia*, 9.

45.   One incident in the ministry of Jesus is particularly instructive. When Christ is confronted with a woman caught in the act of adultery[99] he does not condone or excuse her offence. But he manifests his trust in the redemptive power of mercy by forgiving the woman, saying to her: "Go and sin no more." And as a prelude to that he focuses attention on the hypocrisy of her accusers, saying: "Let him who is without sin cast the first stone." Jesus was here not operating within the formal framework of the law. This was not a court but there were statutory codes of jurisprudence which required a specific penalty: that the woman be stoned to death. Jesus sets these aside, again prompting questions about the difference between legal and divine justice and about when forgiveness and compassion are more important than retribution. In this Christ more fully reveals a God who is "rich in mercy".[100] Mercy is contrasted with God's justice, and shown to be "not only more powerful than that justice but also more profound".[101] God's total love is given not because we have earned it, but because we need it.

46.   How are we to apply this to the criminal system in our own time? The question is problematic. Mercy, as Jesus showed, is necessary for justice to complete its personal and social end. It does not abolish the order of justice but is the freedom to transpose justice into redemption. It is what makes society humane. Yet because it is not bound by any law, it operates as a personal and intimate act of the moral imagination and it is difficult to see how this can ever be reduced to an abstract principle. How, then, do we institutionalise mercy within our criminal justice system?

47.   It is important to say that mercy is not to be confused with weakness. As Pope John Paul II reiterates: "In no passage of the Gospel message does forgiveness, or mercy as its source, mean indulgence towards evil, towards scandals, towards injury or insult. In any case, reparation for evil and scandal, compensation for injury, and satisfac-

99 John 8:1-11.
100 Ephesians 2:4.
101 Dives in Misericordia, 4.

tion for insult are conditions for forgiveness."[102] The Christian option is not the soft option. We are instructed to love our enemies[103] and love, in the definition of Aquinas,[104] means seeking the good of the other. Yet this, as every parent knows, is not the same as being lenient or permissive. We have, therefore, to consider what is the best way to show love to those convicted of a criminal offence

THE PHILOSOPHY OF PUNISHMENT
48. By what right does our society deprive people of their liberty? Criminologists generally offer four justifications for punishment. It is to exact retribution; to remove criminals from society and restrain them committing further crime; to deter others from committing the same crime; and to reform offenders.[105] The general assumption is that these various intentions, are to a considerable degree, simultaneously achievable in an attempt to balance an acknowledgement of the moral culpability of the criminal with the possibilities of reform and rehabilitation. It is worth considering whether this is indeed possible.

RETRIBUTION
49. The word 'retribution' has picked up pejorative connotations in common usage. There is something about it that smacks of the vindictive and the primitive. It is important, therefore, to strip away this emotional undertone. Philosophically the rationale of retribution is the restoration of the social equilibrium which the offence disturbed. The

102 *Dives in Misericordia*, 14.
103 Matthew 5:44.
104 *Summa Theologica* 2a2ae. q.1. Aquinas accepts this definition of Aristotle but recognises that for the Christian it cannot be complete. It comes within the discussion of "friendship" whereby the love of friends is a mutual seeking of each other's good. However, for Thomas we must expand beyond mutuality to love even those who do not love us (e.g. our enemies and sinners) for God's sake.
105 The Criminal Justice Act 2003, spelt out five elements in its definition of sentencing: the punishment of offenders; the reduction of crime, partly through the deterrent effect of penalties imposed; the reform of offenders; the protection of the public; and reparation for offences committed. But it makes no suggestion on which of these are appropriate with different offenders in differing circumstances.

primary purpose of the punishment which society inflicts is as Pope John Paul II puts it "to redress the disorder caused by the offence".[106]

50.   In this approach to punishment the concept of desert is central (see para 18). Since individuals are free moral agents who must take responsibility for their actions, those who offend against what society deems to be acceptable deserve to be punished. (There can be, of course, as in the case of unjust laws, situations in which acts which are illegal are not wrong, and there is a significant tradition in Catholic thinking about justice and law and when it is appropriate to break the law in good conscience. But where morality and the law coincide the principle of desert on issues of crime and punishment is a central one). It is worth underlining that the principle of desert also insists that this retribution must, in the degree and character of the punishment, reflect the seriousness of the offence. Our criminal law is predicated on the assumption that society excludes and diminishes offenders with similar force to the violence of the crime they have committed. Punishment is immoral if it is disproportionate or contains any element of vindictiveness.

51.   The classic expression of this ethic of retribution is the Old Testament lex talonis: an eye for an eye, and a tooth for a tooth. But in addition to retribution this also embodies the principle of proportionality, that is to say only an eye for an eye, only a tooth for a tooth. Or, as Shakespeare put it, when justice demands a pound of flesh, it requires exactly a pound of flesh.[107] The prohibition on unlimited revenge is reflected in a long Judaeo-Christian tradition of taming the instinct of vengeance. Punishment is legitimate, but as penal reformers like Jeremy Bentham argued, must be proportionate and unnecessary suffering must be minimised. Popular phrases which express the principle of retributivism, "the punishment must fit the crime", "just deserts" and the like, can all be regarded – contrary, often, to general usage – as demonstrating balance and proportionality, ruling out sentences which are too harsh as well as those which are too soft. In such an approach punishment is not meant to be reformatory.

106 Evangelium Vitae, 46, quoting The Catechism of the Catholic Church, 2266.
107 The Merchant of Venice.

52.   Those who argue that retribution is the primary purpose of imprisonment could logically argue that the guilty should be punished even if this achieves no consequential good. Such an approach is generally rejected in favour of a more utilitarian outlook in which "what actually works?" is seen to be the prime question to address. One of the reasons a retributive approach has fallen from favour is the perception that it does not work when it comes to making society safer. Being tough is not necessarily synonymous with being effective. Yet it is worth noting that such empiricism contains an ethical difficulty. A purely utilitarian outlook must reject notions of "just deserts" and yet desert is central to society's right to deprive a person of their liberty: offenders are punished because what they did is wrong, not simply because it is convenient for the rest of society. The punishment must also be seen to "fit the crime" whereas, under a utilitarian approach it would be legitimate to argue for severe penalties for even small crimes to maximise their deterrent value. We shall return to this when we come to consider the balance between individual rights and the common good. Retributivism is now intellectually out of fashion, and yet its concept of desert emanating from the key notion that we are all responsible for our actions, is not one which our society can afford to discard.

INCAPACITATION

53.   Another traditional justification for incarcerating criminals is that prisons eliminate the immediate threat to the rest of society simply by removing offenders from circulation and placing them where, while they are behind bars at any rate, they can do no further damage. There is a superficial attraction to that argument, when it works in combination with the retributive principle of desert; without that it would justify locking up suspects without due process – which is one of the reasons why **the current British Government practice of using immigration regulations to detain, without trial, foreigners suspected of terrorism is deeply questionable.** (There are serious *prima facie* human rights violations involved in this.) **The Government needs to reconsider its approach here.** Indeed present penal practice relies on the justification of incapacitation when a prisoner is held for

longer than the crime itself merits, primarily for the safety of the public.[108]

54.   The principle of incapacitation becomes alarming when large portions of the prison population are merely "warehoused", as is inescapably the case at present. This is of particular concern when – despite all the rhetoric about reform and rehabilitation – what most prisoners actually experience amounts to little more than incapacitation through containment. Prisons without hope are mere storage pens, as the Catholic bishops of Ontario recently put it. The purpose of sentencing ought to be to contribute positively to a well-functioning society, rather than just to achieve control and damage limitation. Our present penal policy is tantamount to a sentence of banishment and little more. And in many cases, as Pope John Paul II has noted "detention seems to create more problems than it solves".[109] A philosophy of straightforward expulsion does little to help either the offender or the victim.

DETERRENCE

55.   The idea that the prime justification for prison is that it deters potential criminals is dubious. If deterrence alone were a sufficient validation, this would work even if those punished were not guilty: to say that may sound like a philosophical quibble but it illustrates a key concern about the business of deterrence. "If there were a law prescribing a mandatory death sentence for any driver going through a red traffic light you can be sure that no one, at least no one sane or sober, would commit the offence," as Lord Justice Laws has put it, pointing out that in practice deterrence is always constrained by the proportionality inherent in the principle of retribution.[110]

56.   There is also a powerful practical objection to relying on deterrence as a rationale for the present policy of harsher sentences.

108 See Lord Justice Laws, a Lord Justice of Appeal, The Future of Sentencing, in *Rethinking Sentencing*, a report from the Mission and Public Affairs Council of the Church of England, Church House Publishing, July 2004.

109 John Paul II, *Jubilee Year Statement on Prisons*, 3.

110 Lord Justice Laws, *op. cit.*.

There is little research on the efficacy of deterrence; rather it proceeds from a common-sense assumption which is hard to evaluate. It may well be that deterrence is more of a pious hope in the minds of those who live reasonably pleasant day-to-day lives than a practical reality. "Fear of imprisonment may deter those who have a job, a home and a family but not those who have no hope of achieving or retaining them," as the last Chief Inspector of Prisons, Sir David Ramsbotham wrote after five years in the job.[111] There are a significant number of criminals whose behaviour seems impervious to "deterrence" or the boundaries of normal behaviour in a prison regime designed to punish and contain; rather they emerge from what have been called "universities of crime" more criminally skilled, more resentful or angry and more psychologically disposed to offend. **A far more effective deterrent than severe sentences**, as the Lord Chief Justice, Lord Woolf, has pointed out, **is increasing the chances of the criminal being caught**. The Carter Report has stated that there is no evidence that a 15-month sentence is any less effective than an 18-month sentence in terms of reducing reoffending.[112]

REFORM AND REPARATION

57.   Of all the justifications for punishment the one which insists it should be for reform and rehabilitation seems most obviously to coincide with a Christian anthropology. But it is worth noting that even where good and effective rehabilitative programmes are in place they do not constitute in themselves a sufficient justification for imprisonment. Were that the case such programmes could be infinitely extendable – which would offend against natural justice.

58.   There are inadequacies in all the theories on which society traditionally justifies the basis of punishment. None of the usual justifications is enough in itself. This is important because political discussions on penal policy often revolve around considerations of

---

111 Prisongate: the shocking state of Britain's prisons and the need for visionary change, The Free Press, 2003.

112 The Carter report: Managing Offenders, Reducing Crime, Patrick Carter, Correctional Services Review, December 2003.

which of these four criteria should be dominant. Yet this is a false question. It is like asking someone who is hungry, thirsty, cold and tired whether they most need food, water, warmth or rest. All of us hold ambivalent or even contradictory views on prison. We know that prison is destructive, and yet we want it to reflect our outrage at the seriousness of certain crimes. Society wants to be simultaneously both punitive and merciful but our overriding impulse is what has been called "our addiction to vengeance".[113]

59.   Some sociologists suggest that the explanation for this lies in the different ways individuals conceptualise the issue at different times. Society's attitudes to crime and punishment are kaleidoscopic and change according to how the question is framed, but the key question is whether the four standard aims of punishment are competitive or complementary and whether the inadequacies in one approach can be said to balance out those of the other three.

60.   Specific circumstances suggest that this catch-all approach fails different groups in different ways. The needs of young offenders are very different to those of prisoners on remand. The responsibilities of women in prison can differ significantly from those of men. Short-term sentences have traditionally been supposed to have more deterrent value than reformative purpose – which is why short-term prisoners are moved from one prison to another so much and almost never given any reformative assistance. Moreover the deterrent effectiveness of short sentences is increasingly being challenged by criminologists. Long-term prisoners have very different needs, not just in terms of basic skills training and drug or behaviour therapy, but also in terms of the maintenance of hope and the creation of a sense of purpose. Which is why **there should be a greater range of prison regimes for different prisoners**. Nor does it seem safe to assume that what deters a prisoner from the prospect of reoffending automatically coincides with what deters potential criminals from offending in the first place. The

113 Tim Newell, former prison governor, Restorative Justice in England, in *Rethinking Sentencing*, a report from the Mission and Public Affairs Council of the Church of England, Church House Publishing, July 2004.

gathering of empirical evidence clearly has something important to offer – but so does the perspective of Christianity.

CHRISTIAN PRIORITIES ON PUNISHMENT

61.   In John's Gospel Jesus places the authority of Pilate to pass sentence on him under the authority of God.[114] But what does this mean in practice? When Jesus took up the scroll in the synagogue of his home town on the day that he inaugurated his public ministry the text which he read was from Isaiah:

> The Spirit of the Lord God is upon me,
> for he has anointed me
> to bring the good news to the poor.
> He has sent me to proclaim liberty to captives,
> sight to the blind,
> to let the oppressed go free,
> to proclaim a year of favour to the Lord.[115]

In this list, proclaiming liberty to captives is the instruction which falls most uncomfortably on modern ears.

62.   In this passage Isaiah may have had in mind the Israelites being set free from slavery in Egypt. Or perhaps he was thinking of those returning to their homes from exile in Babylon. Or he may have been referring to those Jews who had sold themselves into service to their fellow Israelites in years of poor harvest and whom the Jewish scriptures decreed were to be liberated every seventh year, with the cancellation of all debts in the 49th year, the Year of Jubilee.

63.   But with Jesus that meaning was enriched. The biblical injunction to set the captives free became an instruction to liberate people from all that enslaves them – from their own sin as well as others' oppression. In today's penal system that imperative covers a wide range of imprisonment, in some cases to free physically

114 John 19:11.
115 Luke 4:19.

individuals or categories of offender who would be better punished outside of prison, in other cases to help liberate those in prison from the social and psychological conditions which have nurtured their criminality. In each case the paramount criterion must be what leads the individual and society towards redemption.

64. That is not to say that certain individuals should not be in prison. The protection of the public requires that dangerous individuals should be physically constrained. The commandment to love our enemies does not necessarily involve us in doing what they want, but rather in making a judgement about what is best for them – ideally a judgement with which the prisoner will eventually come to agree. The business of liberating captives can be as much about how we treat those who are in prison as well as about considering whether certain offenders should be behind bars at all. The answer to the question "by what right does our society imprison people?" is a complex one. It is that society has a duty to the common good which involves public protection, a right to deter those who are tempted to rip further the social fabric, and a responsibility to reform and rehabilitate those who have offended.

65. The insight into the relationship of justice and mercy is what Christian reflection brings to society's questioning about justice and punishment. The Christian understanding of the purpose of punishment cannot be one that is purely punitive nor deterrent. As we have seen, the thrust of the Judaeo-Christian tradition, made most explicit in the ministry of Jesus, insists that the primary aim of any penal system must be to reform and restore. **Punishment should contain retribution, in its best and most balanced sense, but more importantly it must be reformative and rehabilitative.** Moreover justice should be restorative and involve reparation which addresses the condition of both victim and perpetrator, since both stand within the dynamics of justice and mercy, hope and forgiveness.

66. One of the most profound illustrations of the relationship between justice and mercy, Pope John Paul II tells us, lies in the parable of The Prodigal Son,[116] despite neither the words "justice" or "mercy" appearing anywhere in the text. It shows, he says in Dives in Misericordia, that mercy springs from the sinner rediscovering his or her human dignity and beseeching forgiveness. Again mercy is not sought as of right but through an appreciation of rights having been forfeited. Mercy is not implored by third parties but is provoked by the repentance of the person who has erred. That mercy unites the beneficiary and the bestower. "It becomes more evident that love is transformed into mercy when it is necessary to go beyond the precise norm of justice."[117] When this happens, the person who is the object of mercy does not feel humiliated, but rather found again and restored to value:

"Mercy becomes an indispensable element for shaping mutual relationships between people, in a spirit of deepest respect for what is human, and in a spirit of mutual brotherhood. It is impossible to establish this bond between people, if they wish to regulate their mutual relationships solely according to the measure of justice. In every sphere of interpersonal relationships justice must, so to speak, be "corrected" to a considerable extent by that love which, as St Paul proclaims, "is patient and kind" or, in other words, possesses the characteristics of that merciful love which is so much of the essence of the Gospel and Christianity."[118]

67.   This contains an important insight for both victim and offender. For the precondition of mercy is that the offender does not *deserve* some advantage; he or she has nothing to demand as of right. Understood in this way, mercy might perhaps be less offensive to the family of a murdered child when that murderer is released. 'Mercy is manifested in its true and proper aspect when it restores to value, promotes and draws good from all the forms of evil existing in the world and in man,'[119] the Pope says. It also offers an important insight

116 Luke 15:11-32.
117 Dives in Misericordia, 5.
118 Dives in Misericordia, 14.
119 Dives in Misericordia, 6.

for the rest of us. Responsible citizens, like the prodigal's older brother who kept the faith, may baulk at a merciful reaction from authority, yet this instinct, though understandable, should not be decisive.

68.   In other words where claims of retribution and redemption conflict Christian mercy dictates that it must be the latter which takes priority. Some secularists will dispute this, saying that this order of priorities is by no means self-evident. Yet Christians know, as in the parable of the Good Shepherd[120] who abandons 99 sheep to go in search of a single lost animal, the priorities of a self-giving God can seem strange to men and women. "Although justice is an authentic virtue in man, and in God signifies transcendent perfection," says the Pope, "nevertheless love is 'greater' than justice: greater in the sense that it is primary and fundamental. Love, so to speak, conditions justice and, in the final analysis, justice serves love."[121]

The story of Frank Cook (part II)

When Frank Cook burst into tears he crossed a threshold of understanding which marks the beginning of real therapeutic activity. Frank Cook believes that the corrupted values of his friends and family set him into a criminal career, and that this deviancy was confirmed by his experiences of penal institutions before he went to Grendon. But in his autobiography[122] he puts his finger on something much more than simple deviancy amplification. He describes something deeper and far more resonant. "You can't love yourself and go around hurting people. It doesn't work like that," he writes. "You hate yourself and that's why you hate everything else."

Love had been missing all his life. "I can't remember kissing my mum or cuddling her. My father was evil and wicked, but she should have got us away from there." Elsewhere he says: "I can safely say that I have never been in love in my whole life. Mums and dads give love – mine didn't." Significantly he comments that "the first person that I felt love from was Dr Gillett."

That was the beginning of a process which led him to the point where he says "the life of a gangster no longer held any appeal. I could make a difference and actually help people, which was a new and satisfying experience for me. Against all the odds I had become a

120 Matthew 18:12-14; Luke 15:3-7.
121 *Dives in Misericordia*, 4.
122 *Hard Cell* Matthew Wilkinson (1998).

role model and that brought with it responsibility." It was not exactly love, but it was the closest Frank was able to get at that point. He was released from jail in 1996 at the age of 43 having spent all but 16 years of his life in some form of institution. The years since then have been far from easy, but thankfully he has been crime free. He was, he says, "filled with the determination to succeed". So far, he has done precisely that.

II: The Individual and Society

The story of the man with the ironing board (part I)

One rainy morning a prison visitor was moving through Brixton prison. She was on C wing, a busy wing which the prisoners refer to as The Fours because it has four levels. She walked up the stairs, looking for a prisoner on the top level who had requested a visit. As she climbed the prisoners stepped aside saying "Good morning, Miss" or "How's it going?" or just "Hi" but everyone she passed said something or nodded.

Everybody was out of their cells. She looked around. There were men in clusters and milling around, rolling up cigarettes, drinking tea from huge blue plastic mugs, shouting and talking. It was difficult to move around. Then she noticed a man ironing at the very end of the level. Without any conscious intent the visitor negotiated several groups of men hanging around cell doors and walked up to him.

"Good morning," she said

He looked startled.

"Good morning"

"I'm wondering if you can tell me where John Smith is?"

"Yes. He's over there."

She turned and there, out of the sea of heads, was the man she had come to see. "Thanks," she said.

"Who are you?" the ironing board man asked.

"I'm a counsellor. I come to Brixton to talk with people."

"How do I get to see you?"

"Well, I can put your name down."

"Yes. Put my name down, please. I would like to see a counsellor. I've never heard of one before!"

She wrote down his name and then went over to see her client.

THE RIGHTS OF THE INDIVIDUAL

69.   Human beings have a range of obligations and rights. Some of these are bestowed by the mutual agreement of society. But others are inherent to us as individuals. When considering questions of crime and punishment it is important to have a clear understanding of which rights and responsibilities are conferred by society and which are intrinsic to us.

CONFERRED RIGHTS

70.   As individuals we inhabit a variety of different spheres. Our identity or "status" is defined by that sphere, and these definitions can vary from one sphere to another. What it is possible for us to do, and to claim, will vary from one area of social activity to another. For all the talk about ours being a "consumer society" our obligations and rights will vary depending upon whether that sphere is education, health, immigration, shopping or the more general framework of the law. The state imposes different kinds of relationships between itself and citizens in different areas. These relationships, and the status they confer and regulate, may also be determined differently at different times and there will always be a measure of fluidity in their construction and application depending on the nature of the society and the various pressures on it or expectations it has. Asking "by what right" and "who decides" in different circumstances is part of the business of political debate.

INTRINSIC RIGHTS

71.   A major strand of the Christian theological tradition is summed up in the idea that every individual is created in the image of God (*imago Dei*). This has given to Catholic social teaching a clear focal point: the human person is the clearest reflection of God that we have. And because God became flesh, and entered the human race in person in Jesus Christ, as true God and true man, Christ challenges us to see God's presence in our neighbour, especially the neighbour who suffers or who lacks what is essential to human flourishing. In relieving our neighbour's suffering and meeting our neighbour's needs, we are also serving Christ. For the Christian, therefore, there can be no higher privilege and duty. As our 1996 document on *The Common Good* put it:

> We believe each person possesses a basic dignity that comes from God, not from any human quality or accomplishment, not from race or gender, age or economic status. The test therefore of every institution or policy is whether it enhances or threatens human dignity and indeed human life itself. Policies which treat people

as only economic units, or policies which reduce people to a passive state of dependency on welfare, do not do justice to the dignity of the human person.[123]

72.   Biblical justice contains a bias towards those who are poor, marginalised or vulnerable. Catholic social teaching therefore contains a "preferential option for the poor".[124] Scripture tells us we will be judged by our response to the "least of these",[125] in which we see the suffering face of Christ himself. Humanity is one family and the vulnerable are not a burden; they are our brothers and sisters. We must always keep in mind that, whatever their offence, every criminal is also a sister or brother for whom Christ died. This notion – that the human individual has an irreducible status which is not at the disposal of the State and in which all rights and obligations are ultimately grounded – is, of course, not particular to Christianity. It is a view of human dignity shared by Judaism and Islam and by many people of good will. Yet it draws unique sustenance from the doctrine of creation, further developed in Christian revelation about the person and work of Jesus Christ. Ultimately, it gives each person an integral status which is beyond that contingently conferred by the state.

73.   This insight has a number of ramifications. It is important to remember that it applies as much to the victim as to the prisoner. It also bears upon our responsibilities as well as our rights: the imago Dei constitutes the basis of obligations to others – for we all carry the obligation to see God in all others, recognising and honouring them – irrespective of wealth, power, prestige, utility or behaviour. Just as justice will concern us with the fitting assignment of duties as well as rights and benefits, so mercy must reveal to us that a new possibility for being human resides in that imago Dei. In the arena of criminal

123 The Common Good and the Catholic Church's Social Teaching, Catholic Bishops' Conference of England and Wales, 1996, para 13.
124 The phrase came out of a meeting of the Catholic bishops of Latin America, held in Puebla, Mexico in 1979.
125 Matthew 25:40.

justice this will self-evidently mean that certain types of behaviour by the state, for example torture, can never be countenanced. But it will also mean that a penal policy which is essentially or primarily punitive is also unacceptable – for it does not fully respect that the human person remains always open to the possibility of mercy as the necessary complement to justice and to the fulfilment of social relations.

THE RIGHTS OF SOCIETY
THE COMMON GOOD

74. Society has rights too. Catholic social teaching addresses this fact in its concept of the common good. By this is meant the whole network of social conditions which enable human individuals and groups to flourish and live a genuinely full human life. As Pope John XXIII put it in his encyclical *Mater et Magistra*, it embraces "the sum total of those conditions of social living, whereby human beings are enabled more fully and more readily to achieve their own perfection".[126] Or as the Catholic commentator Paul Vallely put it: "It does away with the old black and white distinction between selfish action and altruistic action. We each contribute to the common good because we want to live in a society which is fair and just. If it is fair and just to others it will be fair and just to us too. We do not have to agonise about our motives, nor bribe or excuse ourselves with concepts like enlightened self-interest. The service of the common good is an end in itself."[127] All are responsible for all – and not only as individuals but also collectively, at the level of society or nation.

75. The common good is the sum of all those social conditions which allow the human dignity of each individual to be respected, and their basic needs to be met, while at the same time giving each man and woman the freedom to assume responsibility for their own lives. The common good requires a stable, secure environment within which each human being can develop their own life as autonomous individuals in a harmonious community.

126 *Mater et Magister*, 1961.
127 Paul Vallely in *The New Politics, Catholic Social teaching for the 21st century*, SCM, 1998.

76.   **Governments therefore have a responsibility to ensure, at every level, local and central, that their policies serve the common good by protecting the weak and vulnerable**, and by promoting the integral human development of everyone. The need for this is singularly urgent in a society where materialism is pervasive, where the bonds of mutual responsibility are being weakened, where moral norms are being eclipsed and where family life is fragmented. **Voters have a responsibility to hold the Government to account on all this.**

77.   In *The Common Good* The Catholic Bishops of England and Wales said:

"The first duty of the citizen towards the common good is to ensure that nobody is marginalised in this way and to bring back into a place in the community those who have been marginalised in the past. The alternative is the creation of an alienated 'underclass' , bereft of any sense of participation in or belonging to the wider community. The existence of such an 'underclass' can never be regarded as a price worth paying in return for some other social advantages to be enjoyed by the majority."

78.   This has particular resonance when it comes to issues of crime and punishment. Here the demands of the common good require that public authorities do all they can to prevent crime and to safeguard people and property, and where offences are committed to hold those responsible to account and to care for the victims. Yet this cannot mean that the needs of the majority are allowed to overrule those of the minority. In a pluralistic and diverse society an advantage for any one group would be morally wrong, as the philosopher of law John Rawls has reminded us,[128] if that advantage does not in the long run benefit the most highly disadvantaged elements of that society. That includes anyone who is vulnerable, powerless and at a disadvantage – be they people on low incomes, disabled, ill or infirm, homeless or poorly-housed, refugees or those in prison.

128 John Rawls, *A Theory of Justice*, 1971.

79.   In the spirit of good citizenship all members of the Catholic Church must accept their full share of responsibility for the welfare of society. The discharge of those responsibilities is no less important than fulfilling our religious duties, indeed they are part of them.[129] Consideration of the common good must require us to keep in mind all those who suffer: the victim and their family, the person punished and their family, and those involved in the administration of the justice and penal systems and our wider society.

FALSE PERCEPTIONS OF THE COMMON GOOD

80.   The common good is not 'the greatest happiness for the greatest number'. At every point the rights of the offender must be protected if they are not to become the victim of the unrestricted claims of a community. What most people want on questions of criminal justice is not necessarily right, as is evidenced by opinion polls on capital punishment. What Pope John Paul II has said on this subject has a wider application here. The death penalty, he says in his encyclical *Evangelium Vitae*, is justifiable only "in cases of absolute necessity, in other words, when it would not be possible otherwise to defend society".[130] He continues: "Today, however, as a result of steady improvement in the organisation of the penal system, such cases are very rare, if not practically non-existent."[131] In the same encyclical he elaborates: "Modern society in fact has the means of effectively suppressing crime by rendering criminals harmless without definitively denying them the chance to reform."[132]

81.   The inference to be drawn is clear here: in a system of penal justice which is in line with human dignity – and thus, in the end, with God's plan for man and society – the primary purpose of the punishment which society inflicts must both defend public order and ensure people's safety, while at the same time offering the offender an incentive and help to change his or her behaviour and to be

129 *The Common Good*, 15.
130 *Evangelium Vitae*, 56.
131 *Evangelium Vitae*, 56.
132 *Evangelium Vitae*, 27.

rehabilitated. This does not mean punishment first and then rehabilitation if there are resources, time or the political will. It requires both, as an integrated purpose. Good penal practice should "correspond to the concrete conditions of the common good" and be "more in conformity to the dignity of the human person".[133]

82.　　　One danger must be guarded against here, both in terms of Government policy and, more generally, in how the rest of us regard those in prison. It is the risk of turning offenders into scapegoats. It is as well to remember that this phenomenon has its roots in a religious practice. In Old Testament times the scapegoat was an animal which was symbolically laden with the sins of the community and then driven out into the wilderness. In our time it is not animals which are the subject of such symbolic demonisation but people. Our media-driven society has a proclivity to light upon certain individuals – notorious criminals figure prominently in this – and make them "the other", offer them up and send them out into a social no-man's-land. This process is about denying the full humanity of an individual and reducing them to their offence. Those who have offended most grievously must not be conceived as "other" but rather as a living example of the potential evil which lies in every heart and against which every soul must be vigilant.

83.　　　Christ insisted on the opposite of this scapegoating. In his parables and encounters he pointed to the danger of the tendency to create "us and them" categories. By his death he demonstrated that even those on whom society inflicts its most loathed and despised punishment have value. He insisted that when individuals or groups embark on the diminution or oppression of anyone – setting ourselves up as judges, condemning, excluding and acting violently against them – we expose ourselves to judgement. All individuals contain within them the potential for good and evil; in all individuals both are manifest in some degree. We deny this when we brand

133 Evangelium Vitae, 56.

others "evil" in their person rather than in their offence. In doing so we flatter ourselves dangerously – for the corruption we condemn in others, we need to acknowledge, lurks within us too. We must remember this: in the only prayer which Jesus taught us, the "Our Father", we are all enjoined to consider ourselves both as trespassers and trespassed against. We are all victims, but we are all offenders too. Indeed, as the Catholic theologian James Alison has pointed out,[134] Christ revealed that one of the truest kinds of faith is that found by those who can undergo demonisation without resentment. In the words of the Archbishop of Canterbury, Rowan Williams, "salvation does not bypass the history and memory of guilt but rather builds upon it."[135] The transforming hope of redemption comes out of sin.

THE FEARS OF SOCIETY

84. Much of our society's response to crime and punishment issues is not based in the hope of redemption but in the experience of fear. Yet the evidence is that much of our fear is poorly founded. Many of the truths which the general public holds to be self-evident about crime turn out to be myths. Ask most ordinary voters and they will tell you that crime is rising, crime is violent and that everyone is now at risk of random attack in their home or on the street. Yet the facts are that crime is falling; it is down 30% since 1997.[136] Most crime – 80% of it – is not violent.[137] And the statistics for burglary show that those who are most vulnerable are single-parent households, the homes of the young, and those in poor inner city areas, while the figures for violence show that those most at risk are not the elderly or the middle-class but young men aged between 16-24, single parents, those in rented accommodation and the unemployed.[138]

85. Yet perceptions of growing crime and insecurity are fostered by both politicians and the media. The recent increase in the severity

134 *Faith Beyond Resentment*, Darton, Longman and Todd, 2001.
135 *Resurrection: Interpreting the Easter Gospel*, Darton, Longman and Todd, 2002, p6.
136 Carter report, *op. cit.*, quoting Table 7.2, Criminal statistics England and Wales 2001, Home Office.
137 British Crime Survey, 1998.
138 British Crime Survey, 1998.

of sentencing was blamed by the Carter Report specifically on the interaction between public perception, media, politicians and sentencers.[139] Successive governments have either cultivated or acquiesced in a simplistic equation between deterring crime and longer sentences when they know that the reality is far more complex. They know that measures to prevent crime, or to increase the rate of detection of those thought to have committed crimes, or to increase the proportion of those who can be justly prosecuted – would all do more to protect the public from the effects of crime than would longer sentences. In our society politicians who promise tough and decisive action on crime nowadays gain political advantage. As a result the main political parties increasingly attempt to "out-tough" one another on law and order. And because this "penal populism" thrives on misunderstanding, honest politicians are sometimes at a disadvantage. Two decades of an increasing party politicisation of the issue of law and order appear to have only made matters worse.[140] **All our political parties have a responsibility to guard against irresponsible exploitation of fears over law and order to gain electoral advantage.**

86. The role of the media must also be brought into question here. The power of the media to help the authorities in the identification of suspected criminals is welcome. This does not mean, however, that the rights of those accused of crime should be compromised in the interests of the media or the wider public. On a broader front the media play into, or even feed, public fear of crime at a time when crime is actually falling.

---

139 Carter report, *op. cit.*

140 "Ministers' reaction has not, on the whole, been to look for new ways of reducing crime or of repairing the damage, but to try to make criminal justice itself 'more effective'. As well as seeking to improve efficiency by reducing delays and increasing detections and convictions, their policies have widened the scope of the criminal law, extended the reach of the criminal justice process, and tightened its grip. Successive governments have introduced legislation to create new criminal offences at a rate of between 100 and 150 offences a year." David Faulkner, The Reform of Sentencing and the Future of the Criminal Courts, in *Rethinking Sentencing*, a report from the Mission and Public Affairs Council of the Church of England, Church House Publishing, July 2004.

87.   The problem is twofold. Some parts of the media, most particularly tabloid newspapers, offer a distorted version of the truth in their selective and sensational reporting of crime. The most dramatic examples of this are to be found in the reporting of murder cases, especially where the victims are children. As bishops we do not shirk from using the term "evil" to describe some deeds and the force behind them. Yet we have grave misgivings about the readiness of some newspapers, and even some politicians, to invoke the term "evil" too lightly to demonise individual human beings. Apart from being unjust to those concerned, the loose use of the term in inappropriate contexts undermines the seriousness with which evil needs to be countered. Human beings cannot be separated facilely into good and evil. Of course, it is in the disturbed nature of those responsible for the most demonic acts that they can deem themselves, even in the heinousness of their crimes, to be in the right. No individual is the sum total of the worst acts he or she has ever committed. Greater sensitivity is needed in the language society uses about crime and criminals; everyone should take care to brand the crime rather than the criminal − labelling an individual a murderer, a shoplifter or a paedophile confuses the two, and can lead us to blur the distinction between those who have committed a one-off offence and those who have a propensity to offend again in this area. Greater clarity on such issues would be helpful.

88.   The second problem is one of context. Focusing only on the most dramatic elements of criminal justice distorts the realities of a complex system. Indeed, the media focus on the most infamous crimes too often distracts us from attending to the mundane work of the criminal justice services with those involved in the whole gamut of crimes. Similarly, television in its drama and entertainment output, rarely depicts life behind bars in anything except the most brutal caricature of the daily reality which members of the Church encounter in our prisons.

89.   The selectiveness of the media here has undoubtedly contributed to the unfortunate politicisation of criminal justice in recent

years with the result that the public tend to over-estimate crime-rates, under-estimate the severity of actual sentences passed, and over-estimate the utility of punishment. Common public views that judges are too lenient (or at the other extreme sometimes too severe) are unrepresentative examples which are published because they are peculiarly horrifying, or at the other end of the scale, trivial. The distorting impact this has on public opinion becomes evident when members of the public are invited to take part in sentencing exercises; in these members of the public – when given sentencing guidelines and a series of different case scenarios – tend to make decisions remarkably similar to those actually imposed by the courts. Revealingly, the proportion of population who say sentences are "much too lenient" has fallen recently from half to a third,[141] indicating that less weight should in any case be given to the tabloid hue and cry on issues of crime and punishment.

90. Responsible broadcasters, journalists and politicians need always to maintain a distinction between proper vigilance and scare-mongering. **Politicians, newspaper editors and TV drama executives who promulgate punitive views, in wilful disregard of the evidence, to gain political or commercial advantage – or who seek to reinforce prejudices rather than convey the overall truth – do a great disservice to the cause of justice and should be held accountable for their actions.** By contrast the Church should applaud those who demonstrate a continuing commitment to painting a more rounded picture of the scale of crime and the scope of punishment. When, for example, a penal institution (a prison, a place for young offenders, or for sex offenders) or, beyond the prison or probation services, a mental health hospital or a reception centre for asylum-seekers is planned for a locality the debate should not be conducted in terms of tabloid cliché responding to uninformed or ill-informed fears. Instead a debate should be fostered which eschews simplistic solutions in favour of those which acknowledge the complex interaction

141 The proportion believing sentencing policy to be "much too lenient" has fallen from 51% in 1996 to 35% in 2001, Figure 8.4, Supplementary Volume, *Crime in England and Wales* 2001/02, Home Office.

of issues of crime, order, justice and the common good – and which dismantle barriers to the development of non-custodial sentences or innovative programmes of support for offenders on and after their release.

91.   There needs to be acknowledgement too of the fact that much of the debate on crime and punishment reflects what Rod Morgan, the Chief Inspector of the Probation Service for England and Wales, has called "the ontological uncertainties of the post-modern world" – that is to say "the criminal justice system probably acts as a lightning rod for more general anxieties". Pope John Paul II articulated a similar insight in his encyclical *Dives in Misericordia*, and indicated that the Church has a particular responsibility to speak out against such anxiety:

> Modern man often anxiously wonders about the solution to the terrible tensions which have built up in the world and which entangle humanity. And if at times he lacks the courage to utter the word "mercy", or if in his conscience empty of religious content he does not find the equivalent, so much greater is the need for the Church to utter this word, not only in her own name but also in the name of all the men and women of our time.[142]

THE TREATMENT OF INDIVIDUALS

92.   There are three aspects of the theology of the *imago Dei* which are useful for our considerations. First it has a universality: it does not allow us to make detrimental distinctions on the basis of any social category – victim, criminal, age, racial type, educational attainment, etc. Second, as must by now be clear, the *imago* is not contingent upon a person's behaviour, rather it is a status which they possess as a gift of being. And thirdly the *imago* is not static or inert: it is not just something that persons *are* but also something that they are called to *become*. This means that actions, intentions, and agency are intimately connected to the realisation of the *imago Dei* at both a personal and social

---

142 *Dives in Misericordia*, 15.

level. In this sense, it carries with it a transformational possibility and dynamic. Practical evidence of this can be seen in the fact – which is all too rarely stated in discussions on penal policy – that whatever influences they are subjected to, many individuals with criminal tendencies, once they reach their mid to late twenties, thankfully, grow out of them. Society through its laws, institutions and practices must therefore seek ways to promote those things which assist individuals to realise themselves as the *imago Dei*. This will have consequences for the treatment of those whom the state categorises as both victims and criminals, as well as those professionals whose daily work is within the walls of our prisons.

VICTIMS

93.   We have already spoken in favour of the extension of the current schemes of restorative justice.[143] Victims, too, often have to undergo a transformative journey. Programmes which offer victims of crime the opportunity to participate in the administration of justice can play a vital part in promoting the realisation of the *imago Dei* in the victim. Programmes which require the offender to take responsibility for the harm they have done, and undertake activities to make amends to the victim and the community, can help bring closure for the victim and help resolve the issues of fear, vulnerability, personal security and self-blame which can be part of the aftermath of crime for the victim. Restorative justice draws bitterness and can take away the anger and resentment which lies behind the Chinese saying: He who seeks revenge should dig two graves.

THOSE WORKING IN PRISONS

94.   Reviews which ask how humane British prisons are often neglect to consider those who spend their working lives administering the system. Prison officers, prison doctors and prison chaplains take on a difficult task at society's behest. For many of them the work is a vocation. At all levels, including leadership levels, there are some remarkably dedicated staff for whom the term prison "service" has

---

143 See paragraphs 27–32 above.

real meaning. In most cases those working in prisons are trying to carry out an important vocation conscientiously in extremely difficult circumstances.

95.　　　However, the appalling conditions of many prisons translate into appalling working conditions for these staff. The Lord Chief Justice, Lord Woolf, recently described the overcrowding in our prisons as "a cancer of the system" which means that "resources that could and should be used so much more beneficially elsewhere are swallowed up in what is correctly described as warehousing of prisoners".[144] The additional pressures that causes for prison staff are considerable. **A few prison workers do not rise above these pressures, in which case staff development – or ultimately disciplinary action – must ensure a safe and dignified environment for other workers and for prisoners.** For the rest the sapping of morale is significant. Added to which, in situations such as those where 'life must mean life' and prisoners are robbed of the little remaining incentive to good behaviour the repercussions for the staff can be seriously corrosive.

96.　　　Visitors to prisons often detect a dispirited workforce. Prison officers top every survey of stressful employment. They manifest record sickness levels, the highest in the public sector.[145] There is a high level of staff vacancies. And there has been a high level of staff turnover, most worryingly at governor level, in recent years.[146] Moreover, there have been no fewer than six different prison ministers since 1997.

97.　　　The analysis of those inside the service is disturbing. "There is so much waste in prison organisation that it is impossible to know

144 Speech in the House of Lords, Friday 26 March 2004, Hansard.
145 The average staff sickness rate in 2003-2004 was 13.3%, far higher than other parts of Government service, according to *The Management of Sickness Absence in the Prison Service*, National Audit Office, 2004.
146 In the five years to March just under a third of all prisons (44) have had four or more governors or acting governors in charge. House of Commons written answer 31 January 2003, Hansard.

whether or not adequate financial resources are available," is the conclusion of the last Chief Inspector of Prisons, Sir David Ramsbotham at his departure.[147] So bad was the situation that in 2001 the then Director-General of the Prison Service, Martin Narey, made a speech extraordinary for its candour, in which he said:

> "We have to decide, as a Service, whether this litany of failure and moral neglect continues indefinitely or whether we are going to reform ... I am not prepared to continue to apologise for failing prison after failing prison. I've had enough of trying to explain the very immorality of our treatment of some prisoners and the degradation of some establishments."[148]

There is small evidence on the ground that things have changed much for the better since he said that.

98.   Undoubtedly **some of the workforce in our prisons, including at leadership levels, needs renewal**. But having said that there are some remarkably talented prison governors, men and increasingly women, who have dedicated themselves to one of the least recognised elements of public service. It would be a missed opportunity if some of the most gifted, who are on the point of seeking more rewarding labour, cannot be included more fully in the development of public policy. **The authorities should discern who are the exemplary public servants in this sector and then listen to them and cherish them.** It is an important part of a Christian presence and ministry within our penal institutions to foster and resource the vision of those in the criminal justice system whose daily work is directed towards the transformation of offenders. **At the same time it is important for the authorities to root out those elements within the prison staff whose vision has been corrupted or jaundiced to the extent that it constitutes an impediment to change.**

---

147 *Prisongate: the shocking state of Britain's prisons and the need for visionary change*, The Free Press, 2003.
148 Martin Narey's speech to the Prison Service Conference, 2001.

99. The *imago Dei* is not simply restricted to the soul but also includes the body. The whole person therefore has a right to integrity. Society has a responsibility for the physical and psychological as well as spiritual welfare of prisoners. Not to promote the interests of prisoners would, in the words of Pope John Paul II, "be to make imprisonment a mere act of vengeance on the part of society".[149]

100. Our concern, therefore, is for a range of issues inside our prisons. At the most basic is the indignity which comes from overcrowding. One prisoner recently wrote to the Prison Reform Trust explaining that he had spent five months sharing a cell in which there was "insufficient space to move around, can't walk in a straight line from window to door. Insufficient ventilation for one, let alone two people. Windows do not open. Toilet not enclosed. Less than three foot from toilet when being used by other inmate". Such conditions do not recognise that the prisoner is made in the image of God. Nor does the fact that many prisoners are still locked up for most of the day and some prisoners are locked in their cells for up to 23 hours a day, according to the Prison Reform Trust.[150] **The Prison Service should add to its Key Performance Indicators one monitoring toilet conditions and another concerning itself with the amount of time spent inside the cell.** Another concern is the violence which can be part of the small change of life in jail. There were 5,882 serious assaults recorded in our prisons in the year 2003-2004, a number which meant the Service failed in its target for reducing such violence.[151] Such a climate of violence is a cause for concern for, as Pope John Paul II has observed, "prisons can become places of violence resembling the places from which the inmates not infrequently come [and] clearly this nullifies any attempt to educate through imprisonment".[152]

149 John Paul II, *Jubilee Year Statement on Prisons*, 5.
150 *An analysis of the Prison Service's performance against its Key Performance Indicators 2003-2004*, Prison Reform Trust, August 2004.
151 *HM Prison Service Annual Report and Accounts April 2003 to March 2004*, HM Prison Service. HMSO, London 2004.
152 John Paul II, *Jubilee Year Statement on Prisons*, 6.

101. But establishing a physical regime conducive to human flourishing extends well beyond the physical. Conditions in prisons can be inhuman or degrading not only in their physical awfulness but also if the full range of provision is not there to make a coherent rehabilitative theory of punishment work in practice. In practice prison life runs the risk of depersonalising individuals, because it deprives them of so many opportunities for self-expression. Whether behind bars or in an open prison, inmates lose their job, home, freedom of movement and their freedom to chose their companions. In practice they frequently lose their self-respect and sense of identity, and all too often find themselves adrift from their family. The psychological toll of all this is alarming. In the financial year 2002-2003 there were 105 suicides in prison – almost one third of them within the first week of a prisoner arriving in jail. This is the highest-ever recorded total – up 40% on the previous year – and is clearly a cause for considerable alarm, especially since research indicates poor management has much to do with the problem; changes in the prison system in the United States have cut the suicide rate there dramatically.[153] **The news that August 2004 produced the highest number of suicides ever recorded in a single month underlines that this is clearly an area the UK Government needs to address as a matter of urgency. Strategies based on reducing prisoners' opportunities for self-harm need to be augmented by ones which concentrate more on promoting well-being.**

102. The problem is twofold. Some parts of the media, most particularly tabloid newspapers, offer a distorted version of the truth in their selective and sensational reporting of crime. The most dramatic examples of this are to be found in the reporting of murder cases, especially where the victims are children. In such extreme and exceptional cases it is right to use the term 'evil' to describe some deeds and the force behind them. Yet we have grave misgivings about the readiness of some newspapers, and even some politicians, to invoke the term 'evil' too lightly to demonise individual human beings. Apart from being unjust to those concerned, the loose use of the term in inappropriate contexts undermines the seriousness with

153 Sir David Ramsbotham, former Chief Inspector of Prisons, *Prisongate: the shocking state of Britain's prisons and the need for visionary change*, The Free Press, 2003.

which evil needs to be countered. Human beings cannot facilely be separated into good and evil. Of course, it is in the disturbed nature of those
responsible for the most demonic acts that they can deem themselves,
even in the heinousness of their crimes, to be in the right. No individual
is the sum total of the worst acts he or she has ever committed. Greater sensitivity is needed in the language society uses about crime and criminals;
everyone should take care to brand the crime rather than the criminal –
simply labelling an individual "a murderer" or "a shoplifter" confuses the
two. Greater clarity on such issues would be helpful.

103.   Given that no system of law or criminal justice is immune from
mistakes, and therefore cannot invariably be absolutely assured of delivering justice, offenders must have the right to maintain their innocence
after they are convicted. One of the most difficult cases for any criminal
justice system is where the person convicted of the crime refuses to
acknowledge their guilt. Sometimes this is a sign of deliberate or unwit-
ting refusal to accept the true nature of earlier actions; this is particularly
the case with some of the most dangerous offenders, including many
paedophiles and some murderers. But sometimes, as high-profile "mis-
carriage of justice" cases remind us, this is a sign of innocence. It is vital
that review and advocacy are an important part of any penal system.
**Government ministers should re-examine the inclination for the
parole system to deny early release to those who refuse to "show
remorse" for a crime which they maintain they did not commit.**

THE PASSIVE AND ACTIVE PRISONER

104.   One significant area of concern which the concept of the
imago Dei highlights in our present prison regime is the extent to
which inmates are treated as objects rather than as subjects. Even
where concern is shown for prisoners' welfare it often takes a passive
form. Sometimes this is understandable. A dangerous or depraved
prisoner, as part of their sentence, has forfeited the right to be present
at their own family gatherings of joy and sorrow. Where such a prisoner is given compassionate leave to attend a dying mother at her
bedside or at her funeral that is appropriately an act of mercy by the
authorities. (It would be interesting to see some research done as

to whether such concessions play any part in changing the wider attitudes or behaviour of such prisoners). But it would be a mistake to see this as a matter of justice; it is clearly one of mercy.

105.   Since acts of mercy proceed from the authorities in such situations, the involvement of the prisoners is inevitably passive. But as Pope John Paul II has said: "Our prejudices about mercy are mostly the result of appraising them only from the outside."[154] They do not betoken a relationship of inequality between the one offering it and the one receiving it, nor does mercy belittle the receiver or offend the dignity of the *imago Dei*. The parable of The Prodigal Son reveals that the reality is different: the relationship of mercy is based on the common experience of the dignity that is proper to the human individual.

106.   Yet too often our criminal justice and penal systems – and recent official reviews of it such as the Carter Report and the Home Office response to it – see prisoners chiefly in a passive role. They are people in receipt of the state's services, rather than people who need to take responsibility for themselves and be encouraged to embrace a more active citizenship. They are merely "serving time". Life in prison often contributes to a loss of responsibility among prisoners.[155] They see discipline as a purely external phenomenon, and neglect the need for them to develop self-discipline. Much of the change required here is attitudinal rather than physical. Some prisons operate "Listeners" programmes in which a few inmates are trained on how to offer support to their fellows during difficult times; a few prisons have experimented with prisoners' peer groups which offer mutual support mechanisms in both life inside and in preparation for housing, benefits and employment on release. These have a remarkably empowering effect, but as yet there are too few such groups.[156] At present disempowerment remains

154 *Dives in Misericordia*, 6.
155 Offenders themselves have no responsibilities except to comply with their sentences and the demands that are made on them. See Stephen Pryor, Responsible Sentencing, in *Rethinking Sentencing*, a report from the Mission and Public Affairs Council of the Church of England, Church House Publishing, July 2004.
156 HMP Prison Manchester, Strangeways, has an impressive group on its B wing, which aims to be a drug-free wing.

the norm. **The Government should encourage the development of more Listeners Programmes and prisoners' peer groups and prisoner consultative forums.**[157]

107. One symbolic touchstone of this is that those in prison are also stripped of their right to vote. The disenfranchisement of convicts goes back to the Forfeiture Act of 1870. It is rooted in the philosophical concept of 'civic death', the notion that sentenced prisoners face a form of internal civic exile which involves the withdrawal of citizenship rights. It is a practice which Government ministers have continued to justify in recent times – despite a ruling in April 2004 by the European Court of Human Rights that it violates Article 3 of the Human Rights Act – by suggesting that those who have been removed from society do not deserve a say in how that society is governed: the disenfranchisement, they say, is temporary, legitimate, proportionate and reasonable. The Government has lodged an appeal against the decision of the Strasbourg court.

108. Certainly it is true that, while the right to participate in decisions affecting our lives might be considered an intrinsic one, the right to vote is one which society confers. To speak of voting as an inalienable human right is to overstate the case. However there are reasons in the Christian anthropology of the *imago Dei* why **the right to vote should be restored for convicted prisoners**.

109. The primary causes of crime today, as we have seen, are related to social exclusion. Civic death, under a law dating back more than 130 years, is not an appropriate response to such offending behaviour. Indeed it is only likely to exacerbate the problems in the already fractured relationship between society and offender. Anything which further isolates prisoners already on the margins of society – and encourages their sense of alienation from the community to which they will return when they are released – should be questioned. The ban on voting for sentenced prisoners does not protect public safety nor is it part of an effective deterrent. It is not a means to correct

157 *Having Their Say; the Work of Prison Councils*, Prison Reform Trust, 2004.

offending behaviour. Nor does it assist in the rehabilitation of offenders, and indeed may well serve to disrupt the process of reformation. If anything it is unfair, since the notion of civic death is applied selectively to prisoners; while in prison they continue to pay tax on savings or capital gains that accrue while they are serving their sentence.

110.   More significant however is the need to inculcate in prisoners a sense that they have a continuing stake in the society to which they will return. Encouraging them to play a positive role in shaping their futures by their own efforts and commitment is part of the psychological and spiritual realignment which a truly rehabilitative regime inside prisons should embrace. Voting, and engagement in the course of an election campaign which prisons could encourage, could then be part of the process of preparing prisoners for resettlement in their communities – a process which Anne Owers, the new Chief Inspector of Prisons has concluded that "can still best be described as patchy".[158] Moreover politicians' agendas are determined by votes. There is no incentive for MPs to consider the problems faced by prisoners – such as unemployment and homelessness on release, increasing rates of suicide and widespread drug use – when people in prison are a group with no political voice. If sentenced prisoners had the vote politicians would be forced to take more of an interest in prisons and the issues raised by prisoners. The right to vote is thus not a moral reward, but a tool of rehabilitation.

111.   The truth is that the current ban on prisoners' voting is part of the business of forgetting about prisons and the people in them. Restoring that right would have a positive impact on the processes of reform and rehabilitation. It would symbolically renegotiate the balance between the rights of society and the rights of the individual. And it would restore to prisoners some sense that they have to become the authors of their own transformation. **The Government should withdraw its appeal against the decision of the Strasbourg court which rules that removing prisoners' rights to vote is illegal. The Government should grant prisoners the vote and seek**

158 *Annual Report of the HM Chief Inspector of Prisons for England and Wales* 2002-2003, HMSO 2004, London.

exemption only in the most serious of cases, where disenfranchisement would be seen as an appropriate penalty for the crime.

112.   We may conclude by quoting the words of a Catholic bishop who formerly had special responsibility for prisons: "The criminal is a threat so we must restrain him. He is a misguided delinquent so we must reform him. But as a human being we salute him – he is a son of God and our brother in Christ."[159]

The story of the man with the Ironing Board (part II)

Many months later Angela Hall, the counsellor from the Prison Advice & Care Trust, and the man she had met by chance at the ironing board, had been working together for a considerable time. He had told her about his life – and a painful life it had been, of abuse, neglect and deprivation. He began to come to terms with the past and was able to have a different sense of what could be his future. His work with Angela had been trying to deal with rage he had inside, the reasons for it and ways of diminishing anger that had been so corrosive to him and others around him.

One day he said to her: "Do you know, I think God sent you to me. That day when you came to The Fours there were loads of men on the wing and yet you walked all that way past them down to me at the end and spoke to me. I was really shocked. I didn't know why you asked me. You had to be sent to me."

---

159 The Criminology of Christ, Bishop Augustine Harris, address on the centenary of Her Majesty's Prison Commissioners, Westminster Abbey, 1978.

III: Hope and Redemption

The story of a killer forgiven

A man was serving a life sentence for manslaughter. He had been a difficult and violent prisoner for years and had spent a considerable time in prison punishment regimes. Then one day almost out of the blue, he received a visit from a member of the victim's family. Because the majority of killings are committed by someone known to the victim the dead person's family knew of the whereabouts of the prisoner. The visitor had come specifically to tell the killer that the family had forgiven him for what he had done.

The visit, and the announcement of forgiveness made during it, brought about a great change in the prisoner. He became much calmer and more amenable. It was as if a great weight had been lifted from him. In due course it was deemed safe to move him to less secure conditions.

GRACE AND THE CONSTANT POSSIBILITY OF CHANGE

113.   When we say that every individual is made in the image of God we are saying something about our essence. But we also speak about our potential. The human being is never a closed or determined entity. There is a proper freedom which belongs to each of us, which is the source of our moral status, our creativity and is also the grounds of our responsibility to God, ourselves and to other human beings.

114.   To help us exercise that freedom properly, and act morally, we all are constantly offered God's grace. The possibility of our receptivity to the action of God's grace is ever-present in every human being by virtue of our human nature. However depraved a criminal act, the Christian can never despair of God's grace and therefore of the capacity in even the most dangerous criminal for remorse and rehabilitation. God's mercy and power are always on offer and always potent. The truth of this is evident to Catholics from our sacramental theology, even as we move from Penance to Eucharist so we move from repentance to redemption.

115.   Everyone can be redeemed, which is why **our penal system must provide opportunities for reform and rehabilitation at every stage**

for all those in its care, rather than the mere 10% who at present complete programmes accredited with being effective in reducing reoffending.[160]

116.   The Christian understanding and experience of hope is related to this. It is not founded on a general optimism about human nature but on the sovereignty of God's grace attested in the *imago Dei* both as a grace of creation and secured in Christ, who is the *imago Dei* fully realised. From the Christian perspective, the reality of Christ and the activity of the Spirit hold open for every human being an authentic possibility of realising their end – even when that may be otherwise circumscribed by their situation. Grace has no boundaries. We are always in the presence and opportunities of grace. This places upon every human being the obligation to realise their own nature and fulfil their purpose. This means that the possibility of change is there for everyone. It also places on society the obligation constantly to create the opportunities which will enable each individual to realise that potential, always providing that the fundamental rights, freedoms and dignity of others are also respected.

117.   Within a penal system this means that resources – human, material and educational – must be available to every prisoner to support and enable their development and rehabilitation. But society has another obligation, in addition to the requirement to provide the resources for a penal system genuinely committed to rehabilitation. It also has to recognise individual transformation when it does occur and has a duty properly to receive offenders back into society when they have convincingly reformed. It is commonplace here to talk of prisoners "repaying their debt to society" but it is important to bear in mind that the concept of "debt" is not an adequate meta-phor here. For a start society clearly has, if not a debt, then an equal responsibility towards prisoners in its obligation to offer an environment conducive to reform. But more than that, when com-mercial debts are discharged no change in behaviour necessarily

160 In 2002-03, just 7,647 prisoners completed an accredited offending behaviour programme.

follows; yet here changed behaviour is required from both prisoner and society.[161]

118. The key additional quality which must be at work here is forgiveness, which requires transformation on both sides. Forgiveness goes much further than the act of mercy. Forgiveness is a moral act of gratuitous love that introduces a new opportunity into history and opens up a new possibility in relations between individuals, and between an individual and society. Forgiveness recognises a rupture but refuses to be bound by its logic. It is not about the erasure of truthful memory; it does not deny what has been done or its consequences. But it is determined that the event or action should only positively direct to new future possibilities. Forgiveness, therefore, is concerned to break the cycle of repetitive crime and retribution, in which both the offender and the penal system seem caught at present.

CHANGE INSIDE PRISONS

119. Society has the obligation to provide the wherewithal to make prison a place of reformation not just one of punishment. Then real change can take place in prisons themselves. That means creating a climate which is conducive to human flourishing, and providing the human, material and educational resources to enable the development and rehabilitation of prisoners. It also means that prisoners have the obligation to apply themselves to take advantage of the possibility of change which is on offer.

THE RESPONSE OF THE CHURCH

120. The Church has a longstanding commitment to visiting those in prison. "When I was in prison you visited me,"[162] is one of the

---

161 Peter Selby, Bishop of Worcester and the Anglican Bishop to HM Prisons has suggested that there are difficulties with applying other metaphors or language from finance to thinking on crime and punishment – talk of tariffs, debt, compensation, etc. He argues it skews thinking, much as does using the use of the language of violence (police forces, fighting crime etc) in reducing criminal activity. See Restorative Justice in a Money Culture, in Rethinking Sentencing, a report from the Mission and Public Affairs Council of the Church of England, Church House Publishing, July 2004.
162 Matthew 25:36.

direct statements Jesus makes about the activity of those who will be found at the Last Judgement to have served him. At present every prison is visited by chaplains, Catholic and of other Christian communities and other faiths, at least once a week, though many have a daily witness. In June 2004 there were 139 prisons in England and Wales[163] served by 310 full- and part-time chaplains of all communities and faiths, as well as others who visit prisons on a sessional basis. The churches work in an increasingly ecumenical style inside prison. There are also priests with part-time responsibilities and dedicated members of the Christian laity assisting with regular faith activities and worship as well as with general prison visiting. Prison ministry is the work of the whole faith community and the chaplains have been appointed to represent the community within the penal establishment.

121. The role of prison chaplain is an ambivalent one. The Prison Act places the chaplain firmly within the context of the prison yet, although chaplains are within the penal system, they have a duty to remain critical of it. Chaplains in prison organise worship, bible study, discussion and courses in spiritual renewal and personal formation. But the core of their work is more informal; some of their most important ministry is conducted in casual conversations and passing contacts. Chaplains deal with the spiritual, emotional and human needs of those in their care. All prisoners are seen by the chaplain on reception to the prison, or within 24 hours, many of them in a traumatised state. Arrest is a dehumanising experience and prison exacerbates that. Inmates find their self-esteem is diminished, they lose their identity and become a number, their physical life is basic and restricted. As Pope John Paul II has put it: "prison life runs the risk of depersonalising individuals, because it deprives them of so many opportunities for self-expression."[164] When a chaplain addresses them as an individual of dignity and worth, someone made in the *imago Dei*, that can be the first step on the road to hope and redemption. The chaplain breaks down barriers which are far more profound than prison walls.

163 As of June 2004, Home Office.
164 Message of His Holiness John Paul II for The Jubilee In Prisons, 9 July 2000.

122. The environment for all this is far from easy. As the Church of England's former Bishop for Prisons and its former Chaplain General have put it:

> "Prisons are places of constant movement and noise. They are authoritarian and regimented. They bring together the violent, the immature and the weak-willed. As institutions, they cannot avoid generating anxiety and loneliness. Not infrequently, they give opportunity to the bully and the pretentious. All this makes any ministry in prison a sobering and testing experience. It is front-line work of care and calls from those who undertake it a considerable degree of self-knowledge and a sure grasp of faith and personal value."[165]

Chaplains must balance a sense that the prisoner is both to be supported and also helped to come to a new self-awareness which will involve the offender passing judgement on himself. The chaplain must therefore offer a clear moral framework together with a sense of standing alongside the prisoner. Above all he or she must be a good listener, prepared to take as their motto the words of Ezekiel who ministered to the Israelites held captive by Babylon: "I sat where they sat."[166] To those who ask to come to prison to "bring the prisoners to God", one experienced prison chaplain often replies: "please come, but you may find that God is already here and that often it is the chaplain who has the conversion experience."[167]

123. Chaplains also have a ministry to those who work in prisons. Staff too can be affected by the dehumanising institutional culture of our prisons and can develop a view of human nature which is jaundiced rather than balancing a sense of realism with the possibility of change. Support for staff is a vital part of the chaplain's role in helping create a climate conducive to human flourishing. So too,

---

165 Rt Revd Robert Hardy and Ven. David Fleming in Prison Chaplaincy, in Prison: a study in vulnerability, Church House Publishing 1999.

166 Ezekiel 3:15.

167 Fr Malachy Keegan, HMP Brixton.

occasionally, is challenging the behaviour of prison staff. Chaplains can also act as sounding boards for governors inside prisons, as points of liaison with voluntary groups working with prisoners, and as a vital bridge with the outside world when prisoners are released. The Bishops of England and Wales committed themselves to improving the work of the Church within our prisons.

THE ROLE OF EDUCATION

124.   Education in prison has improved significantly in recent times. There has been an increased focus on numeracy and literacy. Prison Service targets for the number of prisoners achieving skills qualifications were significantly exceeded in 2002-2003, with 41,300 Basic Skills awards being made (43% above target).[168] The Prime Minister has announced that he hopes increased investment in prison education will double the number of educational qualifications achieved by prisoners by the end of next year.[169] This is to be applauded. Research highlighted by the Government's Social Exclusion Unit has found that prisoners who do not take part in education or training are three times more likely to be reconvicted. By contrast basic skills learning can contribute to a reduction in reoffending of around 12%.[170]

125.   Increasing the provision of accredited offending behaviour programmes for prisoners has been one of the Prison Service's priorities. Accredited offending behaviour programmes are based on evidence-based practice and have been accredited as conforming to principles derived from what works in reducing reoffending. The two most widely available programmes are Enhanced Thinking Skills and Reasoning and Rehabilitation which are designed to develop thinking skills, social perspectives and moral reasoning. In recent times questions have been raised over the effectiveness of offending behaviour

168 Carter Report, *op. cit.*, quoting HM Prison Service data.
169 Tony Blair, foreword to the Social Exclusion Unit report *Reducing reoffending by ex-prisoners*, July 2002.
170 Social Exclusion Unit report *Reducing reoffending by ex-prisoners*, July 2002.

programmes. Two recent Home Office studies[171] found no difference between reconviction rates for prisoners who had participated in the Enhanced Thinking Skills and Reasoning and Rehabilitation programmes and for those who had not. The Prison Service has been disappointed by these results and has cut the target for such programmes and diverted resources to drug treatment courses. **The Government should reconsider this. Such programmes should not be seen through a purely utilitarian lens, for education is a good in itself**, and is one of the key tools for realising the potential of the *imago Dei* in each individual. At present there is danger that education in prisons is becoming too narrowly focused on achieving the basic skills targets and not on the needs of individual prisoners. The prisons inspectorate has reported that: "Again and again in education inspections we point to the need to construct education and training plans around individual needs assessments. And the focus on education should not be at the expense of providing recreational and cultural opportunities, which may be the pivotal thing that a prisoner responds to."[172]

126.   But if there has been progress in prison education it is from a fairly low baseline. Half of all prisoners are at or below the level expected of an 11-year-old in reading, two-thirds in numeracy and four-fifths in writing.[173] Yet in 2002–2003 an average of £1,185 per prisoner was spent on education.[174] According to the Offenders Learning and Skills Unit in the Department for Education and Skills, just under a third of the prison population is attending education classes at any one time.[175] The average number of hours prisoners

171 *Understanding What Works: accredited cognitive skills programmes for adult men and young offenders*, Cann J, Falshaw L, Nugent F, Friendship C, RDS Study 226, Home Office 2003, and *Searching for 'What Works': an evaluation of cognitive skills programmes*, Falshaw L, Friendship C, Travers R, Nugent F, RDS Study 206, Home Office, 2003. Quoted in *An analysis of the Prison Service's performance against its Key Performance Indicators 2003-2004*, Prison Reform Trust, August 2004.

172 HM Chief Inspector of Prisons, 2002.

173 *Prison Statistics England and Wales 2002*, Home Office, 2003.

174 Ibid., cost of secondary school teaching is £2,590 per student per year.

175 Ibid.

spent in formal learning activities, for the period September 2002 to August 2003, was just nine hours per week.[176]

127.   These problems are compounded by the current overcrowding crisis. One of the consequences of crowded prisons is the constant juggling with inmates to try to make places available in the jails to which new prisoners are sent. The result is that significant numbers of prisoners are moved from one prison to another. In 2003 there were some 100,000 such transfers. This "churn", as it is known within the prison system, results in a number of problems, mainly affecting those on short sentences. (This is despite the fact that it is these short-term prisoners who would most benefit from interventions; Home Office research indicates that drug misuse is most prevalent among offenders sentenced to less than a year).[177] It is not uncommon for families to turn up for prison visits only to be told that their relative has been moved, sometimes quite considerable distances; one family arrived at Feltham near London recently to discover their relative had been moved to Northumberland.

128.   The consequence in education is that prisoners who have been making good progress in one programme find themselves suddenly in a prison without a programme or in one with a different one, since national parity in delivering programmes is virtually impossible to maintain.[178] The National Audit Office has highlighted the high number of movements of under-18-year-olds between prisons to make way for new arrivals, disrupting education and training courses and leading to inconsistent support and supervision.[179] It is

176 House of Commons written answer, December 2003.
176 Carter Report, op. cit..
177 The Government has acknowledged this. Speaking to the Home Affairs Select Committee in May 2004, the Prisons Minister, Paul Goggins, said: "The amount of movement within the prison system ... makes it difficult to work effectively on rehabilitation and resettlement. People are doing certain courses and then get moved to a different prison".
179 Youth Offending: The delivery of community and custodial sentences, National Audit Office, 2004. The NAO reports that there were 2,400 movements of young offenders alone between April 2002 and January 2003.

hardly surprising therefore that a recent study by the Prison Reform Trust of inmates' own perspectives on education concluded that "despite the highly appreciated efforts of some education staff there was a desultory second-best feel to prisoners' accounts of education".[180] **There is clearly a need for the Government to do more to improve education in prisons and in particular to address the issue of disruption to education programmes caused by the constantly rising number of internal prisoner transfers. There is a need to establish parity in the delivery of rehabilitative programmes throughout United Kingdom penal institutions.**

DRUG AND BEHAVIOURAL TREATMENT

129.   Over half of all prisoners confess that they have a drug dependency problem.[181] That means there are currently more than 40,000 prisoners in need of treatment. But though in 2002-2003 there were more than 40,000 applicants to detoxification programmes for drug misuse (nearly double the target) and although there are highly successful drug treatment and rehabilitation programmes in 60 prisons – aimed at prisoners with moderate to severe drug misuse problems – only 4,386 prisoners entered these programmes in 2002-2003. The target for March 2004 was only 5,700 entries per year. Some allowance needs to be made here for the fact that the Prison Service restricts access to the programmes to those sentenced to two years or more because of the length of the treatment courses which are a minimum of 12 weeks. Even so it is clear that there is a huge deficit between need and provision when it comes to drug treatment in our prisons.

130.   Most prisoners do not receive help with their drug problems. According to the Social Exclusion Unit, officers at HMP Manchester have estimated that 70% of prisoners come into the prison with a drugs misuse problem but that 80% of these have never had any contact with drug treatment services.[182] There is a particular problem with young offenders: nine out of ten young adult prisoners say they

180 Prison Reform Trust, October 2003.
181 54% according to Hansard, 11 June 2002.
182 Social Exclusion Unit report, *Reducing reoffending by ex-prisoners*, July 2002.

use drugs prior to imprisonment but only one in three Young Offender Institutions provide drug treatment programmes.[183] Some of those who do benefit from such schemes find that transfers between prisons due to overcrowding often disrupt drug treatment. Ironically those who are most often transferred are short-term prisoners among whom drug misuse is most prevalent and who would be those who would benefit most from treatment programmes. The result is that drug use on release from prison is very high.

131.   A study by the Office for National Statistics found that about half of prisoners using illegal drugs, and who had been receiving treatment while in custody, reported being offered help to obtain treatment on release. But only 11% had a fixed appointment with a drug agency and four months after their release half were back to using heroin on a daily basis. One Home Office survey of prisoners who had predominantly served short-term sentences, and had used drugs in the 12 months before imprisonment, found that 77% admitted taking illegal drugs since release. With drugs at the root of so much crime these figures are alarming, for they indicate that the prison system is missing the chance to assist prisoners on a matter of particular vulnerability and failing to engage with one of the chief causes of crime when it has people in custody and the opportunity to do so.

132.   That those prisoners who do undergo successful drug programmes in prison find that help melts away when they leave jail is a matter for concern. Treatment and support services in the community for prisoners leaving custody is very limited. Prisoners are often viewed as "new cases" when they are released and have to join the back of the queue for the few community programmes that do exist. The Home Office has no comprehensive tracking systems in place to monitor access to community drug treatment.[184] The recent Government initiative to combine the work of the prison and probation services will go some way to addressing this problem but it is clear that not enough is being done inside our prisons to tackle drug misuse – a misuse

183 Ibid.
184 Written Parliamentary answer, 9 June 2003.

which is both an affront to the intrinsic human dignity of prisoners and the direct cause of much reoffending. We welcome the Government's announcement in September 2004 of the intention to allocate more money to drug treatment programmes in prison. The challenge now is to make sure the treatment in custody is followed with support when ex-offenders are released back into the community.

133.   Many of these concerns also apply to behavioural treatment programmes. The Prison Service in 2003, for the fourth year running, failed to meet its target for the number of prisoners who complete Sex Offender Treatment Programmes. And over 4,000 sex offenders in prison did not undertake the Sex Offender Treatment Programme, with some prisons – such as Dartmoor which houses a high number of sex offenders – unable to offer any sex offender treatment. Such a situation is, as the Chief Inspector of Prisons noted in 2003, unacceptable. This is obviously not a straightforward matter of resources. Among sex offenders there are larger than average numbers of individuals who deny their offence; engaging them in treatment can be a particular challenge. **Even so, this is not an area in which the Government is making sufficient progress, and it needs to examine why.**

WORK INSIDE PRISONS

134.   Catholic social teaching sees work as the quintessential human activity through which men and women "subdue the earth" and share in God's creativity (cf Genesis 1). Work, in the analysis of Pope John Paul II,[185] is the defining act which makes us fully human, for our potential is realised through action, work and by acting in solidarity with others as "a person in community". Work expresses human dignity and also increases it. Meaningful work, he implies, is a basic human right.

135.   In his Jubilee Year statement on prisons in July 2000 the Pope applies this notion specifically to the penal system:

185 See Pope John Paul II's encyclical *Laborem Exercens* (1981).

To make prison life more human it is more important than ever to take practical steps to enable prisoners as far as possible to engage in work which keeps them from the degrading effects of idleness. They could be given access to a process of training which would facilitate their re-entry into the workforce when they have served their time ... Prison should not be a corrupting experience, a place of idleness and even vice, but instead a place of redemption.[186]

It is unfortunate that when the prison system is under pressure – as it is at present as never before in modern history – the first thing to be sacrificed is what is known in prison as "purposeful activity". Purposeful activity includes a wide range of activities such as: education and training courses; employment; induction; resettlement and rehabilitation activities; sports and PE; religious activities and visits. In 2003, despite the efforts of the Prison Service to bring a huge expansion, with an extra 2.5 million activity hours for prisoners, the average number of hours per prisoner did not increase (from 23.2 hours a week) because the huge expansion was absorbed entirely by the increase in the prison population.[187] The Prison Service has now decided to scrap its "key performance indicator" on purposeful activity. This should be retained.

136. What our prisons need is more purposeful activity, not less. The current definition of a full working day in a prison workshop is four hours. The work, by and large, is menial low-skilled and poorly-paid. Much of it is mind-numbingly dull tasks such as folding carrier bags, counting nails or manufacturing huge quantities of socks, slippers and jeans in quantities far greater than the prison service needs for internal consumption and of a quality which would not find a market elsewhere. Such a system is deeply flawed. It pays scant respect to the dignity of the prisoner. It is ineffective in helping the prisoner towards a reform of attitude or towards gaining the kind of skills

186 Message of His Holiness John Paul II for The Jubilee In Prisons, 9 July 2000.
187 Evidence from the Chief Executive of the National Offender Management Service, Martin Narey, to the Home Affairs Select Committee, 25 May 2004.

which would be helpful in rehabilitating them in the outside world. It does little to assist the working of the prison nor to contribute towards the considerable cost to society of running the current system.

137.   Our prisons need a revolution to make work more meaningful. **A full working day should be introduced to parallel that of the outside world, eight hours a day, five days a week. The work too should relate to the outside world, with prisoners learning the disciplines, skills and standards they will need for resettlement when they are returned to society.** Such a system would help inculcate the work ethic which is normal among most of the population, and to which many of those in prison have never been exposed. It would teach them transferable skills. It would pay them real wages, from which they could send money home to their families, pay reparation to their victims and perhaps even make some contribution to their keep.

138.   Such a notion is not utopian. A number of pilot schemes – developed in partnership between the prison service, private companies and charities – have pointed to the viability of such a system. The Mount prison in Hertfordshire has a self-financing printing shop, together with workshops in engineering and electronics, and plans for a bricklaying course. Prisoners are here doing real work for real contractors to real standards. The Road Haulage Association, with its industry short of 50,000 workers, is looking to train and employ prisoners. National Grid Transco, which needs more than 3,000 new gas engineers in the next five years, has run a pilot in a young offenders' institute to train and employ prisoners which has been so successful that it is to be extended to more institutes and prisons. To date, more than 80 inmates have qualified from the Transco scheme and some 70% found employment; only five were reported as reoffending. Contrast that with the general situation whereby 75% of prisoners leave prison without a job and 70% are released with no education, training or employment.[188]

188 Social Exclusion Unit report, *Reducing reoffending by ex-prisoners*, July 2002.

139.   There will be complicating factors. There will be issues about the balance of the local job market. There will be concerns from trade unions if competition from prison shops is perceived as unfair (though it may be that jobs, such as those in administration and call-centre work which are currently being "out-sourced" abroad, could be done in prisons with prisoners being paid and taxed and beginning their process of rehabilitation). There may be ethical issues about private companies profiting from prison labour, though they already do from running private prisons in the first place and it is hard to see why private sector activities in prisons should be any more questionable than firms making a profit from health or education. **But, once such matters are resolved, such pilot schemes should be extended nationwide making the employment of ex-offenders much more attractive to employers than at present.**

140.   Such an approach would also make more viable the concept of clusters of community prisons which was advanced by Lord Woolf in his 1991 report on prisons after the Strangeways riot. Following Home Office research showing offenders who maintain links with their families are six times less likely to reoffend, his proposal was for each region of the country to have a cluster of sufficient prison places to hold all the various types of prisoner. If each area had its own cluster of prisons – high security, training, resettlement, women's and young offenders – the system would be able to customise its care for different types of prisoner, reducing the dehumanising institutional-isation which goes with the modern trend towards larger prisons, and also enabling prisoners to keep in contact with their families as well as allowing community involvement in their rehabilitation and resettlement.[189] All of this, research shows, would reduce rates of reoffending. Such an approach would be more consonant with Christian concerns about human dignity than the suggestion, made

189 Successful work is being done in such areas in places like HMP Latchmere House in Richmond, Surrey which prepares men serving life sentences for release by allowing them day release to jobs in the local community. But such resettlement prisons are few and the regimes within them in need of improvement, according to Latchmere House: a report by HM Inspector of Prisons, Home Office, 28 November 2003.

in the Carter report,[190] that old and unsuitable prisons should be replaced by larger institutions, providing better value for money. **The Government should set out a timetable for moving to the system of clusters of community prisons.**

USING PRISON LESS

141.   Faced with the many inadequacies within our prison system it might be argued that the solution is simply to spend more public money on the system – building more prisons and then staffing, equipping and resourcing them properly. Regardless of the cost to the taxpayer, it might be argued, society has the need to lock more people away for its own safety and security while at the same time ensuring that those offenders undergo proper reform and rehabilitation programmes. Many people will disagree with this notion simply on grounds of cost: spending on prisons and probation has already increased by over £1bn (in real terms) in the last decade to £3.5bn, which is public money which might well be better spent elsewhere. Others will point out that other countries manage without this, reminding us that for every 141 prisoners the UK holds in prison Germany has only 98 and France just 93 without those European countries being less lawless or unsafe as a result. Indeed crime levels in Britain and the other major Western European countries are broadly comparable. But a Christian anthropology will go further. For there are clear arguments for suggesting that the principles of justice and mercy, of human dignity and the common good, insist there is a need for our society to change our thinking on the use of custody. **Building more prisons is not the answer.**

142.   Some 70% of those in our prisons are there for non-violent offences. In 2001 some 42% of women convicted of motoring offences in the Crown Court went to prison (compared to just 8% a decade earlier). In 2002 around 40% of women imprisoned were sent down for shoplifting, theft or handling stolen goods.[191] Since the

190 Carter Report, *op. cit.*, section 9.
191 *Reducing crime, managing offenders*, Patrick Carter, Correctional Services Review, December 2003.

containment and incapacitation of such criminals is not the primary grounds for their imprisonment there must be a case for considering whether alternatives to custody are not more appropriate for a significant number of prisoners.

143. The traditional assumption which underlies our national penal policy is that punishment progresses through a graduated response, starting with fines and moving – where fines do not work – to community service, and thence for those offenders who do not respond by changing their ways, to prison. The underlying philosophy is that a custodial sentence is, so to speak, the default position for every offence.

144. The political slogan which epitomises this approach is: Prison works. On this basis governments, of both parties, have introduced measures making increased use of custody. Mandatory sentences have been introduced, after a third offence, of three years for burglary and seven years for certain drugs offences. This was in response to evidence which showed that, previously, the average sentence for a third offence of burglary was just 17 months, with 19 months for the seventh offence. This went some way towards satisfying public outrage; burglary is a crime which arouses strong public opinions – 83% of burglary victims report being emotionally affected, with 11% suffering depression and 12% panic attacks. In international surveys England and Wales has one of the highest proportions recommending custody for a convicted domestic burglar.[192] Since a relatively small number of people were responsible for the majority of burglaries, the aim was to target an easily identifiable criminal group. As a result someone convicted of a first-time offence in burglary had a 48% chance of receiving a custodial sentence by 2000, compared with just 27% in 1995/96. At the same time, the average sentence length had increased from 16 to 18 months.[193] And yet the Carter Report has shown that tougher sentences have only a limited

192 Carter report, *op. cit.*
193 Ibid.

impact on crime: the increased use of prison is estimated to have reduced crime by around 5% out of an overall fall in crime of 30% since 1997.[194] And the reconviction rate for burglars is still 75%.[195]

145. So if, as this demonstrates, prison does not work, then what society needs is less of it, not more.

146. There are both practical and philosophical considerations here. The Government's new Sentencing Guidelines Council started work in early 2004. Part of its remit is to study sentences and relate them to what happens to those sentenced after release, to discover which sentences work, and which appear not to, in terms of preventing reoffending. Its members must study the relative merits of prison and probation to ascertain when, for example, a fine may be more effective with a low-risk offender with a low probability of reoffending, than might be a community sentence order or prison. But already most penologists accept that short sentences are largely ineffective, and may indeed be counter-productive, since three to four months in prison is not long enough to offer any serious rehabilitative work and yet is long enough to lose an offender his or her job and home, promoting the likelihood of reoffending. It is alarming that the current increase in the use of short sentences is at the expense of community penalties or fines.

147. **The Sentencing Guidelines Council should be given the brief not simply of rationalising and systematising sentencing so that it becomes proportionate, consistent and effective. It should also be given the brief of gearing the system so that fewer people are sent to prison.** It might start by recommending that large numbers of very low risk offenders be diverted from prosecution by conditional cautions, warnings and reprimands. It might consider how to reduce the needless use of custodial remand. Above all it might look at ways to reverse the inflationary tendency which has crept into sentencing.

194 Carter quoting Table 7.2, Criminal statistics England and Wales 2001, Home Office.
195 Prison Reform Trust, Feb 2004.

148. Sentence inflation has a number of causes. Some are complex sociological interactions between public fear, media sensationalism, political perception and the anxiety of judges not to seem out of touch. But some are linked to the Government's increased use of mandatory sentences. Fixed tariffs – for murder the shortest possible life sentence will now be 15 years and for most firearms offences, five years – appear to have a tidal pull, raising sentences across the board. As sentencers aim to achieve proportionality in their sentencing thresholds are inevitably pushed upwards. **This is a trend which needs to be arrested and indeed reversed.**

149. But the Sentencing Guidelines Council needs to do more than consider issues not simply from a utilitarian standpoint. It must also ask which sentences best balance effectiveness with the maintenance of the human dignity of the offender. A Christian anthropology will have something to say here on issues such as whether sentences should, for the most part, reflect the gravity of the individual offence or whether they should take more account of the persistence of the offender. In the public mind the former is the more common perception; it is what underlies notions such as the "punishment fitting the crime". Talk of what is "the appropriate penalty" carries retributive undertones of prison seen primarily as punishment. But if we are to see prison – in line with a Christian vision of justice and mercy – as a place where rehabilitation should take precedence over retribution then **it may not be appropriate for sentences to reflect, first and foremost, the gravity of an offence. Rather they should be a response to how probable it is that any punishment other than prison is likely to fail.** This makes sense both in pragmatic terms and in response to considerations of human dignity.

150. In part this is saying that society should divert the lowest risk offenders out of the prison system and punish them in the community. It suggests that other offenders should better be punished through restrictions of liberty in the community than through short prison sentences. It insists that **custody should be reserved for the most serious and dangerous offenders**. But it does more than all this. It challenges the philosophy that takes us steadily and inexorably through a graduated hierarchy of punishment to the conclusion that prison is always the answer.

FINES

151.   Over the past decade the use of fines as a punishment by courts has fallen by a quarter. In 1991, 1.2 million offenders received a fine but by 2001 this had fallen to 900,000. The fall was in direct and inverse proportion to the rise in prison sentences. For more serious offences, the fall in the use of fines has been even greater, over 30%. Those inside the criminal justice system are wont to talk of a "collapse" in the fines system. This reflects two things: the increased severity in sentencing, and a perception that many criminals simply refuse to pay fines and that the system is insufficiently rigorous in following-up to collect them. The problem here seems psychological rather than philosophical, for there seems no reason why, with sufficient political will, a new drive could not be injected into the system to rebuild fines as an effective strategy, **using new systems such as computerised direct deductions from wages and reinvigorating old enforcement strategies** which make effective more severe punishments for those who fail to pay fines. It will take political and administrative effort, but **the fines system should be rebuilt**.

152.   It should not, however, be inevitably seen as the line of first recourse for the courts. Many fine-defaulters come from the social group who are not in work and are in receipt of benefits. Previously the strategy with such defaulters has been to dock their benefits. This strategy is questionable. If state benefits are fixed at a level which gives recipients what is considered the bare minimum needed to live in our society then it is unacceptable to make deductions from this. It is an assault on human dignity to expect people to attempt to survive on less than what is acknowledged to be the bare minimum. Society's provision of the basics of life to those in need is not contingent upon some notion of moral worth, but rather on considerations of some intrinsic right, which Christians will describe as the *imago Dei*. From a pragmatic point of view, deductions from survival benefits creates an incentive to crime. It is a social strategy which is setting itself up to fail. **For the poorest in society fines should not be courts' first recourse; sentences of community service, in the form of unpaid work or some acts which focus on paying back to the community, make more sense, as part of a much more comprehensive system of community sentencing**, on which more below.

153. For most members of society there is much to be said in the reconsideration of the idea of Day fines. Under this a fine is set as a number of days and the offender then must pay in proportion to what he or she earns in an average day. Offenders can either pay in a lump sum, in instalments, or opt instead to work for the community. Those failing to pay face a prison sentence based on the number of unpaid days. This means that punishments would impact upon offenders in direct proportion to their means to pay. It creates a new transparency in sentencing as well as an effective deterrent and punishment. This is a system which has been briefly piloted in the UK in the past,[196] but in such a way as did not properly gauge the practicality of the notion, allowing certain anomalies to arise – huge fines for trivial offences, and trivial fines for serious crimes, in certain cases – which a better-thought-through approach could avoid. Day fines should be restricted to offences that would go to court. Fixed penalty and minor offences would be excluded thus avoiding excessive fines for very low-level crimes. Day fine systems are used successfully in several parts of Europe; in parts of Germany, 80% of criminal sentences are Day fines. **The Day fines system should be introduced in the UK.**

---

196 A similar system was successfully piloted in the late 1980s and early 1990s in four courts. The well-publicised high fines for minor offences were because (in certain highly untypical cases) courts fined unemployed offenders as though they were at the top of the earnings scale in the absence of means information. But the fault was not in the legislation, as set out in the Criminal Justice Act 1991, but rather because it was applied without common sense by some courts. In general the experiment led to a higher number of fines being imposed, better tailoring of fines to offenders' means and a lower rate of default which ought to have been accounted a success.

DISCOVERING ALTERNATIVES

154. The system of community service at present available in England and Wales is fairly limited. Government has recently made some attempt to extend it, renaming it community punishment. In part this is a response to complaints that the old community service was not tough enough. Indeed some critics have maintained that it is ineffective since the type of offender who often refuses to pay fines also refuses to turn up properly for community service programmes, which are inconsistently enforced, or else attend them with an attitude which is so chaotic and truculent as to render the system meaningless. But, if community punishment programmes are insufficiently effective at present, that is a problem of implementation rather than one of inappropriate conceptualisation. **We would like to see a wider range of community punishment programmes which encompass everything from courses to promote a sense of social responsibility to schemes of punishment which are as onerous, if not more demanding, than the present system of time spent idly in prison. Prison would be reserved for those who are dangerous or who violate the conditions of punishment programmes.**

COMMUNITY PUNISHMENT

I.   The Carter review suggested that the Government makes greater use of rigorous alternative sentences. The Criminal Justice Act 2003 creates a generic community sentence, that will allow the court to tailor a community punishment to offenders' needs by picking and mixing from a range of interventions – drug treatment, offending behaviour programmes, community service, tagging etc. New programmes to exemplify this approach are already being introduced. Among the enhanced community punishment schemes is an Intensive Control and Change Programme (ICCP) which is being piloted for 18–20-year-olds to provide a range of interventions targeted at the specific needs of young adult offenders. It includes tagging, curfew and police surveillance options, as well as providing 18 hours a week of offending behaviour programmes, employment and training.[197]

197 Carter report, op. cit., 4.

II.   The sentencing powers of magistrates have been expanded by introducing three new sentences – Custody Plus and Intermittent Custody (which include terms in prison) and Custody Minus (a form of suspended prison sentence that allows for up to two years' supervision in the community). The intention is that these sentences will replace the use of short custodial terms of up to six months (in 2002 more than half of those sent to prison were there for jail terms of six months or less).[198] All this is a welcome alternative to prison.

III.   The implementation of these new sentences, however, raises some concerns. The first is that, though these sentences were designed as alternatives to short custodial terms of up to six months, early indications are that they are being used by the courts for offenders who would otherwise have received a lesser punishment.[199] A form of sentence inflation has already begun. Our second concern is that these new sentences, most particularly Custody Minus, may be set about with conditions such that large numbers of offenders – such as those who have chaotic lifestyles or drug problems – are likely to breach them, causing the offender then to be given a custodial sentence. **The new measures should aim to reduce rather than increase the numbers in custody. The Government needs to guard against the danger that they may do the opposite.**

IV.   **The Government also needs to create lesser levels of punishment in the community. A range of new types of community service should be introduced with particular emphasis on the needs of offenders who are women, boys, elderly or petty offenders or those suffering from mental problems. At the lowest level these should be rehabilitative schemes which do not give the offender a criminal record. For differing offences, and offences of increasing seriousness, programmes with differing emphases should be tailored.** Community rehabilitation programmes should tackle offenders' risk-assessed needs including education, drugs, thinking

198 *Prison Statistics England and Wales* 2002, Home Office (2003), HMSO, London.
199 *Punishment and Politics*, Tory, M, Cornwall: Willan, 2004.

and behaviour. One example of this is a scheme called the Milton Keynes Retail Theft Initiative, launched in 1994, which requires shoplifters to take part in an extensive course that requires them to meet shop-owners who are victims of theft, confront the reasons why they steal, and teaches them skills to move into work and resist peer pressure; reconviction rates fell to just 3%.[200] Another example is the Dordrecht Initiative in Hartlepool in which a multi-agency approach is also used with offenders identified as particularly problematic; based on a successful initiative developed in the Dutch city of Dordrecht, police and probation officers work in concert with a drugs nurse and outreach supporter workers who supervise the offender in a range of training, housing and constructive leisure activities: the result, to date, has been that over half those targeted have not been convicted of any further offence.[201] In programmes such as these different offenders may require basic education skills, or introductions to employment practices which for many offenders may be their first contact with the world of work and its ethic and discipline.

v.   Ideally such schemes would lead to employment which, research reveals, is one of the surest preventatives of reoffending. They would also provide a new engagement with the local community in the form of unpaid work or some acts which focus on paying back to the community offended against. This should be a two-way process. It gives local people some say in the work completed by offenders. And it fosters in offenders the growth of a new feeling of responsibility for others, along with a sense of community spirit and social solidarity.

vi.   Where possible these schemes should incorporate an approach geared to restorative justice, which makes reparation directly to the victim, and indirectly to the whole community. Requiring offenders to interact in that way may build the empathy they have previously lacked. Evidence shows that, where prison can harden

200 The Independent, 9 June 2004.
201 Delivering Neighbourhood Renewal in Hartlepool, Hartlepool Borough Council, December 2003.

individuals, the experience of restitution often softens them and provides the motivation to reform which the prison system fails to give to many.

DRUG TREATMENT IN THE COMMUNITY

VII.   Although drug treatment is difficult, evidence suggests that it can be cost-effective in reducing crime and social harms.[202] Some new initiatives are under way here. The Government has recently introduced a measure called the Drug Treatment and Testing Order (DTTO) as an intensive community sentence to tackle the link between drug use and offending. It involves greater contact with supervision officers, as well as regular drug treatment and testing. In 2002, over 6,000 DTTOs were ordered, under which the offender and his or her probation officer report back every month to the judge or magistrate who originally sentenced them. **This practice could usefully be extended to other community sentences** since it serves the dual function of constituting an incentive to the offender to comply with the order, and also gives sentencers some idea of the efficacy of their various sentences.

VIII.   Despite this initiative, provision of drug treatment is patchy and inconsistent across England and Wales. Given the clear links between drug dependency and offending, **improvements in drug treatments as part of community punishment programmes ought to be a clear priority**, both on pragmatic grounds and on those which take into account the possibility of transformational change. Drugs are a peculiarly piteous assault on the dignity of the human individual and on the realisation of the *imago Dei* which each individual is called to become.

ELECTRONIC TAGGING AND SATELLITE SURVEILLANCE

IX.   Modern technology increasingly offers new possibilities of punishment in the community. Electronic tagging is already

202 Carter report, *op. cit.*, quoting "Economic analysis of costs and consequences of drug misuse and its treatment: two year outcome data from the National Treatment Outcome Research Study", Godfrey, Stewart and Gossop, 2003.

extensively used to manage offenders without removing them from society. Some 70,000 offenders have been tagged under the Home Detention Curfew scheme introduced in April 2003 in an attempt to ease prison overcrowding. Under this scheme, prisoners can now leave custody under electronic surveillance up to four months before their release date. Further possibilities are opened up by GPS satellite technology which is now being successfully used in the United States to provide more detailed monitoring of offenders in the community. The system allows offenders to be tracked 24 hours a day either in real time or with information provided at the end of each day. An alert is activated if an offender departs from an agreed schedule or they enter a zone from which their sentence has excluded them. It is also possible, using the same technology, for probation officers to communicate with offenders at any time.

x.   **The introduction of GPS satellite technology** in England and Wales would be welcome since the system offers a regime which curtails the freedom of offenders in a selective way, allowing them to remain in their home and job and in touch with their local community, while curbing their activity in areas which could be sources of temptation. Such systems allow for a much better balance to be struck between concerns about individual human dignity and public safety than is possible in custody. They would be particularly useful with remand prisoners, one in five of whom are acquitted eventually and only half of whom are ever given a custodial sentence. **The Government needs to guard against the recent tendency significantly to increase the numbers awaiting trial being remanded into custody.**[203] **At present it is doing the opposite: the 2003 Criminal Justice Act reversed the presumption in favour of bail in certain cases.**

155.   In June the Government merged the national prison and probation services into a new National Offender Management Service

203 In 2002, 58,700 people were sent to prison ahead of their trial, a 10% increase on the previous year, according to *Prison Statistics England and Wales* 2002, Home Office (2003) HMSO, London.

(NOMS). The development of this will be observed with interest. There have been those who have suggested that it is a step in the wrong direction; what is really needed, they argue, is a system which is more independent of civil service bureaucracy – something which is a cross between the old Prison Commissioners and the increasing numbers of private prisons. For it is also arguable that the creation of the new integrated NOMS structure could promote rather than hinder the development of a penal system which is genuinely orientated primarily towards reform and transformation.

156.   If it is to succeed, **it is important that the National Offender Management Service encourages greater continuity of treatment of offenders, regardless of whether they are given a custodial or community sentence. It should also allow the possibility of a new flexibility which does not see custody and community punishment as alternatives – a flexibility which is part of what this report would like to see. It should make use of sentences which begin in prison and then move to a punishment and rehabilitation programme within the community, at first in halfway houses and then in offenders' own homes. It should make greater use of curfews and house arrest, surveillance and monitored exclusion orders. It should require offenders to go to prison only at weekends, allowing them to keep their job and home, and maintain their family and community links.**[204] **It should require them to undergo some custodial rehabilitative programme in most of their leisure time.** Such initiatives could not only reduce crime and maintain public confidence but, properly developed, would build a culture more conducive to the theological imperatives which the balance between justice and mercy, human dignity and the common good requires.

CHANGE IN THE COMMUNITY

157.   Finally, it is essential never to forget that the kind of transfor-

---

204 We welcome the announcement by the Home Secretary in a speech on 29 September 2001 to introduce intermittent custody to allow men and women to go to prison at night or at weekends while keeping their job and maintaining their family.

mation which the Gospel requires takes place not just within individuals, nor even with institutions, but within a wider social context. As we have noted, both mercy and forgiveness operate as personal acts of the moral imagination. They cannot be demanded or confected but come as a genuine and unexpected offer and gift. Because of their personal character it is more difficult to reduce them to an abstract principle, in the way that societies do more easily with justice. This means that, in our society, the instruments of hope and redemption will not best be mediated through the official institutions of the state, however humane its penal system becomes. Private initiatives will be required.

158. Employers whether in the private, public or voluntary sector have an important role to play here in the attitude they adopt to the employment of ex-offenders. A recent survey carried out among 550 Human Resource (HR) professionals showed that over two thirds of those who have employed ex-offenders report that it has been a positive experience, only 6% say that is has been negative.[205] The Chartered Institute of Personnel and Development (CIPD) say that this new evidence is a serious challenge to the stereotypical responses and resistance of employers. Many often adopt blanket exclusion policies as they are frightened to take the risk of employing ex-offenders. It is encouraging therefore to find that two thirds of HR professionals think it is reasonable to expect organisations to make a conscious effort to recruit ex-offenders with 40% of their survey respondents saying they would be willing to consider an application from an ex-offender. They point out that given the tight labour market and high levels of satisfaction, the recruitment of ex-offenders can make business sense as well as serving the common good.

159. The Church has a particular role to play in this. Acts of mercy and forgiveness are permanently established in Christian experience through the Cross and Resurrection of Christ and the continuous gift

---

205 *Employer attitudes towards ex-offenders: Survey Report*, Chartered Institute of Personnel Development, November 2002.

of the Holy Spirit. The Christian community is called to witness to this in its actions. At grassroots level this places certain responsibilities on individual parish communities.

160. Some discharge these well at present. Some congregations have schemes in place by which ordinary families can strike up a relationship with the family of someone who is in prison, sometimes merely standing alongside them in solidarity but sometimes adopting a role of mentoring to a prisoner's family offering role models of reliable love. Some offer not only personal support and counsel, but direct people to the resources and services that are available in the community to those in need.[206] Others help with parenting classes in prisons and young offenders' institutions. Yet others offer practical help such as the church in Durham (see Appendix) which has a team of volunteers who make themselves available to meet women prisoners who have no one to meet them on discharge, and after a considerable time in custody are apprehensive about even simple tasks like getting themselves to the railway or bus station. **Direct initiatives at parish level to assist ex-offenders and prisoners' families need to be extended throughout the country.**

161. Other Christians choose to work in charitable groups which are not religious in their overt philosophy. Victim Support has 12,000 volunteers who provide practical help and emotional support for those whose lives are turned upside down as a victim, or witness of crime. The organisation also supports some of those victims who chose to participate in systems of restorative justice which, as already stated above, is a vital area in which the Government needs to expand work. Such schemes, which can be greatly beneficial for both prisoners and victims, can also make considerable demands on victims. Offering support to them before, during and after this process is vital.

---

206 One simple way of doing this is where computer-literate priests or parish information officers help ex-offenders to access provision such as the Community Legal Service which operates through the website http://www.clsdirect.org.uk/index.jsp. The internet can also provide ready information on housing, employment and prisoner rehabilitation services. See Appendix for a list of charities and services.

162.   Others work with statutory bodies such as Local Criminal Justice Boards, in which partnerships of professionals – including the police, the Crown Prosecution Service, magistrates and the Prison Service, the Probation Service and Youth Offending Teams – try to draw the local community and its leaders into positive engagement with those at risk of offending or reoffending, such as those whose siblings have got into trouble. Another such semi-official system is Crime and Disorder Partnerships[207] which focus on tackling drugs and alcohol problems and the anti-social and criminal behaviour they provoke; they work at stifling the availability of illegal drugs on our streets and provide services that enable people to overcome their drug problems and live healthy and crime-free lives.

163.   Other Christians focus on the needs of particular groups. Care Remand Fostering is a project that provides temporary care and accommodation in private homes for young offenders who would otherwise be remanded to custody. Others involve themselves with The Prison Advice and Care Trust (PACT) which, among other things, works with prisoners who have mental health needs. Elsewhere more than 1,000 volunteers are active in 80 prisons, in befriending schemes to support and encourage those separated from their families by imprisonment – assisting prisoner's wives and husbands or working with their children in prison visitors' centres. Others spotlight particular needs: those who work with Parents in Prison offer mothers and fathers in jail the opportunity to record a bedtime story for their child, and add a personal message.

164.   Some work with national bodies like Alpha for Prisons, which over the past two years has linked more than 400 discharged prisoners with individual church congregations in a project which has helped more than 60% of those resettled avoid further conviction and reimprisonment. Some join more local schemes like the Surrey Appropriate Adult Volunteer Scheme which supports vulnerable detainees through the police custody process or the Kensington and Chelsea Volunteer

207 See http://www.crimereduction.gov.uk/drugsalcohol7.htm

Bureau's HMP Wormwood Scrubs project which offers day release opportunities for prisoners in the final year of their sentence.

165.   Yet others work with ex-offenders when they leave prison. Projects from the Catholic organisation the Depaul Trust help young prison-leavers find accommodation before release and match them with one-to-one volunteers for support in linking them to schemes to build educational qualifications or explore employment opportunities. The Kainos Community, whose programme is based on Christian values, though it is open to people of all backgrounds, helps ex-offenders develop life skills through 24-hour community living, learning respect both for themselves and others.

166.   The churches are also helping offenders to reintegrate into local communities, through the development of Community Chaplaincy schemes. Volunteers are recruited from churches and other faith groups, to work under the supervision of a coordinator or community chaplain, in befriending and mentoring released prisoners. In Swansea, one of the first areas where a local scheme was developed – and in London where a scheme has been started to support young offenders – a reduction in reoffending by those supported, has already been demonstrated. Most prisoners simply want someone to talk to and to encourage them. Some schemes are developing drop-in centres, where advice will be available on housing, education and employment as well as from agencies providing other services. Often the prisoners helped are those who repeatedly serve short sentences for comparatively minor offences, and have few community ties. Community Chaplaincy was first developed in Canada, as were Circles of Support and Accountability, which offer a more intensive form of engagement specifically for released sex offenders, who have often been in prison for some years, and may have been rejected by family and friends. Circles work closely with statutory agencies. The Circle meets weekly, and initially there will be some sort of contact with the ex-offender, who is known as the Core Member, every day. If the Circle becomes concerned with the Core Member's behaviour, it will be challenged, and a decision may be taken to share the concern with police or probation. In this country pilot Circles of Support have been funded by the Home Office.

167.   More work should be done in this field since it inverts the process of isolation or, in the case of paedophiles, social ostracism or even persecution by the local community, which all too often reinforces ex-offenders in the pattern of behaviour which created their offence in the first place. The evidence is that "community chaplaincy" significantly reduces rates of reoffending. It seems to us no coincidence that approaches like this, which appear to be successful, are ones which work with the grain of Christian theology rather than against it.

168.   Such ideas in action (for more details see the Appendix) give a sense of what is possible. **Christians need to be encouraged to participate more in such direct practical initiatives to assist ex-offenders, prisoners and their families.** As a Church we have to acknowledge that concern for those in prison is – despite it being one of the baldest of Jesus's commands as to how his followers are to serve him[208] – is not at present high up the agenda of many Christians. There are many reasons why churchgoing Christians might not put criminal justice top of their list of concerns. Some may see the subject as too political, or too radical, while some may feel safer supporting a mission field far from home. Others may make a simple distinction between the deserving and the undeserving, failing to separate the sinner from the sin. We have to confess that many Christians have been heavily influenced by baser instincts, all too often fed by the tabloid press, which seeks to portray prisoners as less than human and not worthy of people's time and energy. We need also to address a common propensity to use concern for victims as an excuse to justify an insufficient regard for how our society treats those it chooses to imprison on our behalf. These are issues which Christian ministers must be prepared to address within their flocks. On this we all need to examine our consciences.

208 "I was in prison, and you visited me." Matthew 25:36.

The story of Bob Turney

Bob Turney's descent into a life of crime began at school where he was labelled a "stupid boy" because of what was, many years later, diagnosed as profound dyslexia. His childhood had been difficult in other ways. His mother was deaf. And when his manic depressive father killed himself, it was Bob who found the body. He was just 10 years old.

From his early years in primary school Bob was labelled as disruptive, uncooperative and lazy. He was treated accordingly, and behaved accordingly in response. When he left school at fifteen he was barely able to write his own name and soon got involved in his first burglary. That lead eventually to armed robbery, just as alcoholism led to drug addiction. He spent the next eighteen years in and out of prison.

His behaviour inside was no better than outside. One fellow inmate ended up with a metal plate in his head after Bob hit him with an iron bar. He became, in his own words, a career prisoner rather than a career criminal. "It offered me a strong sense of security – boundaries I never had in the outside world," he has said. "And although the attention I got was negative, at least it was attention."

Then, one day, 20 years ago, in one of his stints outside jail, Bob regained consciousness in a public toilet. His shirt was covered in blood and both of his wrists were slit. He had been drinking for four days straight. "I was admitted to a rehabilitation clinic after finally acknowledging I had a problem," he recalls. It was only the start of a long slow road to recovery. "The psychiatrist said I was institutionalised and now using hospitals instead of prisons to hide in and unless I changed I would end my life as a long-term inmate somewhere."

Though he had the reading age of a ten year old, he began to tinker with a computer in the office of a rehab charity. He started to write the story of his life. His spelling was so bad that when he put the spell-check on, the computer asked him what language he was using.

But eventually, after sobering up, Bob got an honours degree in forensic social work from the University of Reading. He then became a Probation Officer and is now a consultant to the Probation Service. His book, Going Straight, written with prison rights campaigner and author Angela Devlin, is now a core textbook for the BA in Community Justice Studies at the University of Birmingham.

Now an active member of his local church, Bob works as a consultant, writer and public speaker whose venues have included the Oxford Union, Eton College and the House of Lords. He makes audiences laugh and cry, sometimes with the same sentence. A judge who heard him said that Bob's was one of the most moving talks he had heard in 30 years.

To each audience Bob Turney offers the same powerful message. No matter how despicable their crime, no one is beyond the power of Christ's saving redemption.

Epilogue

169.   When Jesus first appeared, after his Resurrection, to his disciples he did so by passing through a closed door. He entered the upper room in which they were locked away from the outside world.[209] As he entered he brought peace and serenity to the hearts of everyone within. Our task – as bishops, as a Christian community and as a wider society – is to do the same for those who have become the prisoners of crime, or the fear of crime, and also for those who are locked away inside our prisons.

170.   It is up to us to ensure that the prison service offers the continuing opportunities for transformation when the moment comes that the prisoner is prepared to embark on the journey of change. That no matter how hopeless their situation may appear to be, we must never give up on anyone. And that every place can be a place of redemption.

209 John 20:19.

Recommendations

True justice must have an inherent bias toward the marginalised, vulnerable or oppressed individuals in society. So should our criminal justice and prison systems.

VICTIMS

1.1 The first imperative must always be to attend to the victim.

1.2 Government needs to review the lack of transparency in sentencing. Offenders fairly automatically serve less time in prison than the sentence handed out by the court. This is a source of unnecessary hurt for some victims.

1.3 Greater awareness of the physical and psychological problems of victims is needed from all citizens, most particularly those who come into contact with victims of crime either through official agencies or as employers, landlords, neighbours and friends.

1.4 Greater awareness of the needs of victims of crime should be encouraged among Christians at parish level.

1.5 There should be far greater use of restorative justice models within our nation's penal system.

INSIDE PRISON

2.1 Punishment should contain retribution, in its best and most balanced sense, but more importantly it must be reformative and rehabilitative.

2.2 A full working day – eight hours a day, five days a week – should be introduced in prison. The work should relate to the outside world, with prisoners learning the disciplines and skills and standards they will need for resettlement when they are returned to society.

2.3 Pilot schemes – developed in partnership between the prison service, private companies and charities – to make the employment of ex-offenders more attractive to employers should be extended nationwide.

2.4 There is clear need for the Government to do more to improve education in prisons and, in particular, to address the issue of disruption to education programmes caused by the constantly rising number of internal prisoner transfers. There is a need to establish parity in the delivery of rehabilitative programmes throughout United Kingdom penal institutions.

2.5 Enhanced Thinking Skills and Reasoning and Rehabilitation programmes should not be downgraded. Regardless of their impact on reoffending rates education is good in itself.

2.6 The Government needs to allocate more money to drug treatment programmes for ex-offenders as they leave prison. Improvements in drug treatments as part of community punishment programmes ought to be made a priority.

2.7 Behavioural treatment programmes for sex offenders and others need to be expanded significantly.

2.8 The Prison Service should reverse its decision to drop its Key Performance Indicator on purposeful activity.

2.9 The Prison Service should add a system for monitoring the amount of time spent inside the cell to its Key Performance Indicators.

2.10 The Prison Service should add a system for monitoring toilet conditions to its Key Performance Indicators.

2.11 The Government should encourage the development of more Listeners Programmes and prisoners' peer groups and consultative forums.

2.12 The right to vote should be restored for convicted prisoners. The Government should withdraw its appeal against the decision of the Court of Human Rights in Strasbourg which has ruled that removing prisoners' right to vote is illegal. It should seek an exemption only in the most serious cases where disenfranchisement would be seen as part of an appropriate penalty for the crime.

2.13 The news that August 2004 produced the highest number of suicides ever recorded in a single month underlines how urgently the Government needs to address the issue of self-harm. Strategies based on reducing prisoners' opportunities for self-harm need to be augmented by ones which concentrate more on promoting well-being.

2.14 The Government needs to investigate whether members of ethnic communities are more susceptible to being sent to prison than their white counterparts.

2.15 The current British Government practice of using immigration regulations to detain, without trial, foreigners suspected of terrorism is deeply questionable. (There are serious *prima facie* human rights violations involved in this.) The Government needs to reconsider its approach.

2.16 The Government should take steps to reduce the number of women in prison for comparatively trivial offences like motoring offences, crimes arising out of financial problems and debt, and shoplifting.

2.17 Immediate steps should be taken by the prison authorities to strengthen the possibility of maintaining ties between women in prison and their children.

2.18 The Prison Service should add to its Key Performance Indicators – for female and male prisoners – one reflecting closeness to home and facilities to arrange visits.

2.19 All of these factors such as the physical and psychological impact of prison on the children and families of prisoners given more weight by the authorities.

2.20 There are some exemplary public servants working to run and staff our prisons. The new National Offender Management Service should do more to listen to them and cherish them.

2.21 For the few prison workers who do not rise above the pressures to which the current overcrowded system exposes them, there should be more staff development to ensure a safe and dignified environment for other workers and for prisoners. Where that fails it is important for the authorities to root out those elements within the prison staff whose vision has been corrupted or jaundiced to the extent that they constitute an impediment to change.

2.22 The Government should set out a timetable for moving to the system of clusters of community prisons as set out in the Woolf Report. Such prisons are more consonant with the human dignity at the core of a Christian anthropology.

SENTENCING

3.1 The new Sentencing Guidelines Council should be given the brief not simply of rationalising and systematising sentencing so that it becomes proportionate, consistent and effective. It should also be given the brief of gearing the system so that fewer people are sent to prison.

3.2 It might start by recommending that large numbers of very low risk offenders be diverted from prosecution by conditional cautions, warnings and reprimands. It might consider how to reduce the needless use of custodial remand. Above all it might look at ways to reverse the inflationary tendency which has crept into sentencing – a trend which needs to be arrested and reversed.

3.3 Sentences should not automatically reflect, first and foremost, the gravity of an offence. Rather they should sometimes be a response to how probable it is that any punishment other than prison is likely to fail.

3.4 The Government needs to guard against the recent tendency significantly to increase the numbers being remanded into custody awaiting trial.

3.5 The recently introduced measure called the Drug Treatment and Testing Order requires offenders, and their probation officers, to report back every month to the judge or magistrate who originally sentenced them. This practice could usefully be extended to other community sentences since it serves the dual function of constituting an incentive to the offender to comply with the order, and also gives sentencers some idea of the efficacy of their various sentences.

3.6 Custody should be reserved for the most serious and dangerous offenders

ALTERNATIVES TO PRISON

4.1 Building more prisons is not the answer to overcrowding. We need to send fewer people to prison and consider how to make more effective alternative punishments within the community. This would both accord better with a Christian vision of prison and also be better at reducing repeat offending.

4.2 The fines system, which many now feel is enfeebled and discredited, should be rebuilt, using new systems such as computerised direct deductions from wages and by the reinvigoration of old enforcement strategies

4.3 For the poorest in society, particularly those on benefits, fines should not be courts' first recourse; sentences of community service, in the form of unpaid work or some acts which focus on paying back to the community make more sense, as part of a much more comprehensive system of community sentencing.

4.4 A Day Fines system – in which fines are structured to reflect how much an individual earns in a day – should be introduced in the UK.

4.5 The new National Offender Management Service should encourage greater continuity of treatment of offenders, regardless of whether they are given a custodial or community sentence. It should also allow the possibility of a new flexibility which does not see custody and community punishment as alternatives – a flexibility which is part of what this report would like to see. It should make use of sentences which begin in prison and then move to a punishment and rehabilitation programme within the community, at first in halfway houses and then in offenders' own homes. It should make greater use of curfews and house arrest, surveillance and monitored exclusion orders. It should require offenders to go to prison only at weekends, allowing them to keep their job and home, and maintain their family and community links. It should require them to undergo some custodial rehabilitative programme in most of their leisure time.

4.6 The Government should introduce a wider range of community punishment programmes. These should include far less severe community punishments than exist at present, starting with courses to promote a sense of social responsibility and which do not give the offender a criminal record. But they should also include schemes of punishment which are as onerous, if not more so, than the present system of time spent idly in prison. In between a range of new types of community service should be designed with particular emphasis on the needs of offenders who are women, boys, elderly or those suffering from mental problems.

4.7 The judiciary should take care to ensure that new styles of community sentences, which were designed as alternatives to short custodial terms, are not given to offenders who would have previously received a lesser punishment. Early evidence is that the opposite is happening.

4.8 Care should be taken to ensure that new sentences, most particularly Custody Minus, are not set out with conditions such that offenders with chaotic lifestyles or drug problems are almost certain to breach them and end up in jail. The new measures should aim to reduce rather than increase the numbers in custody. The Government needs to guard against the danger that they may do the opposite.

4.9 GPS satellite technology should be introduced for tagging.

PAROLE

5.1 It is inhumane, however horrifying their crimes, to leave prisoners with no hope of release once they have ceased to be a danger to society. The Government should acknowledge this.

5.1 Government ministers should re-examine the inclination for the parole system to deny early release to those who refuse to 'show remorse' for a crime which they maintain they did not commit.

SOCIAL ATTITUDES

6.1 All our political parties have a responsibility to guard against irresponsible exploitation of fears over law and order to gain electoral advantage.

6.2 Politicians, newspaper editors and TV drama executives who promulgate punitive views, in wilful disregard of the evidence, to gain political or commercial advantage – or who seek to reinforce prejudices rather than convey the overall truth – do a great disservice to the cause of justice. They should be held accountable for their actions.

THE CHURCH

7.1 More direct initiatives are needed at parish level to assist ex-offenders and prisoners' families.

7.1 Christians need to be encouraged to participate in the debate on criminal justice and prisons and to apply their faith directly to issues of controversy. Christians need boldly to challenge the myths and prejudices which underlie so much penal populism.

"The mood and temper of the public in regard to the treatment of crime and criminals is one of the most unfailing tests of the civilisation of any country. A calm and dispassionate recognition of the rights of the accused against the state, and even of convicted criminals, a constant heart-searching by all charged with the duty of punishment, a desire and eagerness to rehabilitate in the world of industry all those who have paid their dues in the hard coinage of punishment, tireless efforts towards the discovery of curative and regenerating processes, and an unfaltering faith that there is a treasure, if you can only find it, in the heart of every man — these are the symbols which in the treatment of crime and criminals mark and measure the stored-up strength of a nation, and are the sign and proof of the living virtue in it."

Winston Churchill

Acknowledgements

Thanks go to Paul Vallely, Fr James Hanvey SJ, and Professor Simon Lee for their help in preparing this document. We are also grateful for the advice of Helen Baly of HMP Wormwood Scrubs, Paul Cavadino, Stuart Dew, Myra Fulford, Fr Malachy Keegan of HMP Brixton, Tim Livesey, Rev Dr Peter Sedgwick, Enver Solomon and Charles Wookey. We would also like to thank the Prison Service, the Prison Reform Trust and Nacro for their assistance.

The need for a Christian appraisal of the criminal justice system has never been more timely. This report meets this need splendidly. Churches' Criminal Justice Forum is delighted to be working with the Bishops, and the Catholic Church, in promoting criminal justice as a cause for Christian concern.

Rev Dr Peter Sedgwick, Chair CCJF.

Appendix

SOME VOLUNTARY ORGANISATIONS HELPING PRISONERS AND THEIR FAMILIES

CARE REMAND FOSTERING

A Christian project specialising in providing accommodation for young offenders who would otherwise be remanded in custody. Based in Birmingham, the service works with local authorities' Youth Offending Teams with a telephone referral system, transport to court and same-day placements. A foster-home scheme (which places only one young offender at a time in each home) and an activities programme to meet the young person's individual needs is provided. All young people are moved away from their home area so that they can benefit from a new start and clear boundaries. Results so far are very encouraging; most of the young people complete the programme and go on to receive a community sentence.

www.remandfostering.org.uk

CARING FOR EX-OFFENDERS

During the past two years, more than 400 discharged prisoners have been linked with church congregations through the resettlement work of Alpha for Prisons. At least 60% of those have settled sufficiently to avoid further conviction and reimprisonment. Although Alpha for Prisons began as an evangelical outreach, with Alpha courses run for 30,000 men and women in prison, resettlement now represents a larger part of the organisation's work. Alpha produces a training manual and recommends that churches have an agreement, or contract, with released prisoners, setting out expectations and ground rules. It is hoping to develop a network of local advisors who will help when difficulties arise.

www.caringforexoffenders.org

DEPAUL TRUST

This charity, founded as a Catholic response to the growing number of young homeless people arriving in London, began working with young offenders in 1998 through two projects, Outside Link and One-to-One. Outside Link helps young prison leavers to secure accommodation before release, in order to prevent them from being homeless and vulnerable to reoffending. The One-to-One project matches young offenders about to be released with volunteers who provide support and advice, to help them live independently and be integrated into the community. Both projects have demonstrated a reduced rate of reoffending.

www.depaultrust.org

KAINOS COMMUNITY (KC)

The Kainos Community runs rehabilitative/therapeutic programmes at the Verne prison in Dorset and at Swaleside prison on the Isle of Sheppey. Prisoners volunteer to join these programmes and are expected to stay for a minimum of six months. The basic ethos of Kainos Community is that prisoners develop life skills through 24-hour community living, learning respect both for themselves and others. They gain insight into the way they think, and so are better able to understand their own behaviour and are helped to change. It is a learning experience in which peers and staff give prisoners feedback and support. Although the programme is based on Christian values, it is not a religious programme: prisoners of all faiths or no faith are welcome. Volunteers are an important part of the programme; they range from 25 to more than 80 years of age. There are considerable benefits to the establishments in which KC operates, with improvement in the behaviour of the prisoners. There is also growing evidence that men who have completed the programme are less likely to reoffend.

www.kainoscommunity.org

LOW NEWTON DRIVERS

While working in the chaplaincy at Low Newton women's prison at Durham, Elizabeth McGurk became aware that many women had no one to meet them on discharge, and were apprehensive about getting themselves to the railway or bus station. A plan was drawn up to have a team of volunteer drivers available. Elizabeth spoke about this at three Sunday Masses in her own church, St Joseph's, Gilesgate; she expected maybe six to volunteer, and when 40 came forward she said"I knew this was a work of the Holy Spirit." There have been obstacles to overcome, but the scheme is now working well. Some women have been taken directly to their probation office and hostel, ensuring that they keep appointments which, if missed, could mean immediate return to prison.

THE MOTHERS' UNION

The Mothers' Union is a world-wide Anglican organisation, promoting the well-being of families, through practical projects established by volunteers within local communities. Members seek to offer that same support and encouragement to those separated from their families by imprisonment. Over 1,000 volunteers are active in 80 prisons, in befriending schemes, women's support groups, work with children in prison visitor centres, chaplaincy teams, and facilitating parenting groups or courses. Though the work undertaken by MU volunteers is varied, the needs which they are seeking to respond to are consistently similar: isolation, loneliness and a sense of grief, caused by separation from family and friends.

www.themothersunion.org

NACRO

Nacro is the largest national charity working to prevent crime and resettle offenders. Each year it houses 4,000 offenders and people at risk in its housing projects. It provides education and training for 14,000 offenders and people at risk in its employment training centres. It helps 12,000 prisoners through its prison-based resettlement workers. It advises 18,000 people through its Resettlement Plus Helpline. And it works with 12,000 young people through its youth activity projects. It is a secular organisation but its staff and volunteers include many Christians working alongside people of other faiths and of no religious faith.

www.nacro.org.uk

PRISONERS' PEN FRIENDS

This charity enables people who care about prisoners to make friendships through the post. It provides a secure forwarding service to ensure that addresses (and, if required, names) are not revealed to prisoners. There are guidelines for correspondents to make sure that appropriate security measures are followed, and there is an advice service should any problems arise. When funds permit, there will be a newsletter for all correspondents to share news and ideas. Prisoners' Pen friends is not a specifically Christian organisation, and is emphatically not in existence to attempt to convert prisoners to any religious viewpoint, but many of the volunteers are Christians.
Gwyn.morgan@prisonerspenfriends.org

PARENTS IN PRISON (PIP)

Mothers and fathers in prison are offered the opportunity to record a bedtime story for their child, and add a personal message. Tapes are sent all over the world, with PIP covering the costs. Most PIP volunteers are drawn from churches. At present, there are projects at Leeds, Highpoint in Suffolk, Holloway and Wandsworth in London and Eastwood Park near Bristol.
PO Box 55, Royston, Hertfordshire SG8 5GE.

THE PRISON ADVICE AND CARE TRUST (PACT)

This came into being in 2001 as the result of a merger of The Bourne Trust and Prisoners' Wives and Families Society – PWFS. The Bourne Trust was founded by two Catholic lawyers to provide better services for prisoners and prisoners' families. PWFS was founded when a group of prisoners' wives met together to discuss their problems and to support one another. Their motive for action was one of self-help. The Prison Advice and Care Trust (PACT) works with prisoners who have mental health needs, both male and female, and supports prisoners' families, working towards successful integration of ex-offenders back into the community. PACT provides a free National Telephone Helpline, Visitor Centre management in prisons in the Greater London area and the South West of England, supervised play for children visiting prison, all-day children's visits, counselling

for remand prisoners, and a first night in custody service in HMP Holloway for women with mental health needs.
www.imprisonment.org.uk

PRISON FELLOWSHIP
In this charity volunteers and staff from all Christian communities show the love of Christ to prisoners, prisoners' families and ex-offenders, regardless of their beliefs. Working with prison chaplains, volunteers based in more than 150 local groups provide ongoing support to prisoners. Many befriend prisoners' families and ex-offenders. Special projects are run by trained volunteers and staff. Its Sycamore Tree scheme is a programme for prisoners on victim aware-ness and restorative justice; prisoners hear from volunteers who have been victims of crime and take part in symbolic acts of restitution. Its Angel Tree project organises local groups who raise funds to buy, wrap and deliver Christmas presents to prisoners' children. It is an excellent way of strengthening family ties. The Compass project, based at Highpoint Prison in Suffolk is a six-month Christian values-based programme for prisoners that covers life skills, Christian lifestyle and the arts.
www.prisonfellowship.org.uk

THE PRISON REFORM TRUST
The Prison Reform Trust is the leading prison charity when it comes to research, education and campaigns. It offers advice and informa-tion to prisoners, their families, prison and probation staff, the legal profession, students, academics and interested members of the public. Its quarterly magazine, Prison Report, is the most challenging and influential voice on prison issues. Its annual lecture, conferences and seminars attract high-profile speakers and large audiences. The Prison Reform Trust carries out research on all aspects of prison. Recent studies include: prisoners' views on prison education, the mental health needs of women prisoners, older prisoners, prisoner councils, foreign national prisoners, prisoner votes, and a report into how sentencers make the decision to imprison offenders.
www.prisonreformtrust.org.uk

APPENDIX

THE SURREY APPROPRIATE ADULT VOLUNTEER SCHEME
SAAVS supports vulnerable detainees in police custody. Sixty trained volunteers try to ensure that the person's rights are observed and that they understand why they have been arrested. They also support detainees through the custody process, including the interview, and they encourage detainees to consider taking legal advice (but do not themselves give such advice). The service operates 24 hours a day for 365 days a year and has successfully responded to more than 9,000 calls since 1995. Staff at Custody Centres in Staines, Reigate, Woking and Guildford are supplied with the names of volunteers and call them in turn. The scheme supports young people aged 16 and under, where parents or guardians are not available, and adults who are judged to be vulnerable, mainly through mental illness or learning disability.
www.saavs.org

VICTIM SUPPORT
In 2004 the National Association of Victims Support Schemes marks 30 years of support to victims of crime and witnesses in court. Victim Support is based on the principle that communities need to offer a community response to those affected by crime. Its 12,000 volunteers provide practical help and emotional support for those whose lives are turned upside down as a victim, or witness, of crime. Victim Support finds that its help is often sought by relatives and friends of those directly affected by the crime – for the impact of a burglary, serious sexual assault or bullying, is rarely limited to the individual. Assistance with criminal injuries compensation claims, attending court to give evidence, and having their story and its consequences heard, perhaps repeatedly, are the day-to-day services freely given by volunteers, trained and supported by professional staff.
www.victimsupport.org

WORMWOOD SCRUBS VOLUNTEERING INITIATIVE
The Kensington & Chelsea Volunteer Bureau has been running this pilot project at HMP Wormwood Scrubs for 18 months. It works closely with the Resettlement Team at Wormwood Scrubs to identify

offenders due to be released from the prison within the next 12 months who would benefit from day release voluntary work. Prisoners are helped by volunteers to improve their employment prospects through skills training, befriending and advocacy
www.voluntarywork.org.uk

Based on a list complied by Stuart Dew of The Churches' Criminal Justice Forum for the Church of England General Synod Report on Criminal Justice, 2004

For a comprehensive list of volunteering opportunities see "What Can I Do?" published by PACT (Prison Advice and Care Trust) on behalf of the Churches' Criminal Justice Forum. It can be ordered by post from:

PACT
Lincoln House, 1-3 Brixton Road, London SW9 6DE
Tel: 020 7582 1313
e-mail: info@pact.uk.net

Churches' Criminal Justice Forum
39 Eccleston Square, London, SW1V 1BX
TEL: 020 7901 4878
e-mail: info@ccjf.org.uk

Rethinking Crime and Punishment
11 Park Place, London SW1A 1LP
TEL: 020 7297 4738
e-mail: info@rethinking.org.uk

or can be downloaded via the websites:
www.imprisonment.org.uk
www.rethinking.org.uk
www.ccjf.org.uk

Index

Alcoholics Anonymous 23
alienation 50
Alison, James 53
Alpha for Prisons 96
alternatives to prison 3, 83, 89, 104–6
appeal hearings 8
Aquinas, Thomas 35

Baker, Kenneth 25
basic skills 73–4
befriending schemes 96
benefit payments, deductions from 86–7
Bentham, Jeremy 36
Biblical doctrine 15–16, 31–2
Blair, Tony 73
Blunkett, David 7
burglary 83–4

capital punishment 51
Care Remand Fostering project 96, 110
Caring for Ex-Offenders 109
Carter Report (2003) 10, 39, 54, 64, 82–4, 88
Catholic Church 4, 6–7, 11, 15–16, 28, 36, 51, 56–7, 68, 70, 94, 98, 107
Catholic social teaching 47–9, 78
chaplains 70–3; see also Community Chaplaincy schemes
Chief Inspector of Prisons 21, 26, 39, 60, 66, 78
children of prisoners 28–30, 103
Christian teaching and tradition 4–18 passim, 33–43 passim, 48, 65, 68–9, 81–2, 85–6, 95–8, 104
Churches' Criminal Justice Forum 6
Churchill, Winston 106

'churn' 75
Circles of Support and Accountability 97
citizenship 51, 65
common good of society 49–52, 57, 82, 88, 94
Community Chaplaincy schemes 97–8
community prisons 25, 81–2, 103
community service and community sentences 3–4, 87–94, 102–6
compassionate leave for prisoners 63
Cook, Frank 13, 44–5
cost of Prison Service 10, 22, 82
Crime and Disorder Partnerships 96
crime levels 82
crime prevention 54
Criminal Justice Act (2003) 88, 92
criminology 35, 40
Custody Plus and Custody Minus 4, 89, 106

Dartmoor prison 78
day fines 87, 105
death penalty 51
demonisation 52–3
Depaul Trust 97, 110
desert, concept of 36–7
detention without trial 37, 103
deterrence 37–42, 54, 87
disadvantaged groups 50
distributive justice 14–15
Dives in Misericordia (encyclical) 33, 43, 57
Dordrecht Initiative in Hartlepool 90
drug misuse and drug treatment 8, 22–4, 28, 74–8, 91, 96, 102, 104
drug offences 83, 96

education of prisoners 21–2, 73–6, 80–1, 102

Enhanced Thinking Skills programme 73–4, 102

ethnic minority prisoners 7, 30–1, 102

European Court of Human Rights 65–6, 102

Evangelium Vitae (encyclical) 51

'evil', use of term 55

Ezekiel 72

family relationships 24–5, 28–30

fear of crime 53–6

fines, use of 4, 86–7, 105

firearms offences 85

first-time offenders 9

forgiveness 70, 94

Gillett, Ray 13, 44

God
  names for 32
  see also grace of God; image of God

governors of prisons 59–60, 73

GPS satellite technology 91–2, 106

grace of God 68–9

Grendon prison 13, 44

Hall, Angela 46, 67

Howard League for Penal Reform 10

human dignity 47–9, 52, 81–8 *passim*, 92–4, 103

human rights 37, 65, 78, 82, 103

image of God (*imago Dei*) 47–9, 57, 61–74 *passim*, 86, 92

immigration regulations 37, 103

Incarnation, the 12

Intensive Control and Change Programme (ICCP) 89

Intermittent Custody 4, 89

Isaiah 32, 41

Islam 48

Jesus Christ 11, 16, 20, 33–4, 41–2, 47–8, 52–3, 69–70, 94, 98, 100

John Paul II, Pope 6, 31–8 *passim*, 42–4, 51, 57, 61–2, 64, 71, 78

John XXIII, Pope 49

Judaism 32–3, 36, 42, 48

justice 13–16, 31–4, 43–4, 48–51, 82, 85, 88, 94
  distributive and corrective 14–15
  miscarriages of 63
  for prisoners 20–1
  see also restorative justice

Kainos Community 97, 111

Kensington and Chelsea Voluntee Bureau 96

key performance indicators for the Prison Service 102–3

labelling 55

Laborem Exercens (encyclical) 78

Laws LJ 38

lex talonis 36

Listeners programmes 64, 102

Local Criminal Justice Boards 96

Lord's Prayer 53

love in relation to justice 44

Low Newton prison 111–12

Manchester prison 22, 76

mandatory sentences 83, 85

marginalisation 50

Mater Magistra (encyclical) 49

media reporting of crime 54–5, 98

mental health problems 21, 25–7, 96

mentoring schemes 95

mercy 32–5, 43, 48–9, 57, 63–4, 68, 70, 82, 85, 94

Micah 32

Milton Keynes Retail Theft Initiative 90

miscarriages of justice 63

Morgan, Rod 57

mothers in prison 28–30
Mothers' Union 111
motoring offences 27, 82, 103
Mount prison 80
Muslim youths 31
mutual support groups, prisoners' 64–5

Nacro 10, 21, 111
Narey, Martin 24, 60
National Audit Office 75
National Grid Transco 80
National Offender Management Service
    24, 93, 103, 105
natural law 15
New Zealand 18

Offenders Learning and Skills Unit 74
offending behaviour programmes 73–4,
    78, 89, 102
overcrowding in prisons 7–8, 59, 61, 75
Owers, Anne 66

Parents in Prison 96, 113
parish communities, initiatives in 95, 101,
    106
parole system 3, 63, 106
Paul, St 43
'penal populism' 54, 107
Pius XI, Pope 88
politicisation of criminal justice 54–6
'preferential option for the poor' 16, 48
Prison Advice and Care Trust (PACT) 67,
    96, 113, 116
prison building 8, 82, 104
Prison Fellowship 113
prison population 7–12 passim
Prison Reform Trust 10, 26, 61, 76, 113
prison staff 3, 31, 58–60, 72–3, 103
prison visits 24, 29, 59, 71, 75, 103
'Prison works' slogan 1, 83–4
Prisoners' Pen Friends 113
private sector activities in prisons 81, 101

probation service 77–8, 104
The Prodigal Son 42–4, 64
proportionality principle 36, 38, 85
public opinion 20, 51, 56
punishment 49–52, 85–7
    Christian priorities on 41–4
    fitting the crime 85
    philosophy of 35–40
    see also community service and
        community sentences
purposeful activity in prison 79, 102

Quadragesimo Anno (encyclical) 88

racism 30
Ramsbotham, Sir David 1, 39, 60
Rawls, John 50
Reasoning and Rehabilitation programme
    73–4, 102
reconviction rates see reoffending
reform and rehabilitation 13, 39, 42,
    2, 62, 66–85 passim, 90, 101–2
remand prisoners 3, 21, 84–5, 93, 104
reoffending 10, 14–15, 18, 22, 24, 69,
    73–4, 81, 84, 90–1, 96–8
reparation 17, 19, 42, 80, 91
restorative justice 17–20, 42, 58, 91,
    95, 101
retribution 35–7, 42–4, 70, 85, 101
rights
    of the individual 46–9
    of society 49–53
    see also human rights
Road Haulage Association 80

scapegoating 52
scaremongering about crime 56
sentencing 4, 8–9, 17, 26–7, 38–40,
    53–7, 83–92, 101, 106
Sentencing Guidelines Council 3, 84–5,
    104
sex offender treatment programmes 78

Shakespeare, William 36
shoplifting 27, 82–3, 90, 103
Shrewsbury prison 8
slopping out 8
Social Exclusion Unit 10, 21–3, 73, 76
sociology 40
Solomon 32
subsidiarity principle 88
suicide 8, 21, 28, 62, 102
Surrey Appropriate Adult Volunteer Scheme 96, 115
Swansea 97

tabloid newspapers 55–6, 98
tagging, electronic 4, 89, 92, 106
terrorism 37, 103
torture 49
training for prisoners 79–81
transfers between prisons 75–7, 102
Truth and Reconciliation Commission 18
Turney, Bob 99
Tutu, Desmond 18

'underclass', creation of 50
utilitarianism 37

Vallely, Paul 49
Vatican Council 29
Victim Support 17, 95, 115
victims of crime 2, 15–20, 58, 101
violence in prison 61
voting rights 65–6, 102

Williams, Rowan 53
women in prison 7, 10, 26–9, 40, 82–3, 95
   children of 28–30, 103
Woolf, Lord 3, 25, 39, 59, 81, 103
work ethic 80, 91
work for prisoners 2–3, 78–81, 101
Wormwood Scrubs prison 97, 115–16

young offenders 7, 10, 21, 40, 89
young offenders' institutions 23, 77, 80, 96